MW00653451

TO: _____

FROM: _____

DATE: _____

WOMEN WHO RIDE
LOVING LIFE, HANDLEBARS AND MYSELF

SARAH ANDREAS

Published by WiseWood, LLC.

9246 State Route 250 NW, Strasburg, Ohio 44680 USA
© Copyright 2018 by Sarah Andreas. All Rights Reserved.
Email: author@womenwhoridebook.com • Subject Line: Women Who Ride
Visit our websites:
www.wisewoodllc.com
www.womenwhoridebook.com

No pages of this book may be reproduced in any form without written permission of the publisher. In addition to the copyright on the entire book, Contributors also maintain their individual copyrights of their articles. These may NOT be reprinted without the Contributor's express permission.

Disclaimer: This is not an official publication from any of the motorcycle manufacturers mentioned in this book. The motorcycles named by brand name in this publication, as well as certain names, models, designations, are the property of the motorcycle manufacturers. In this publication they are used for identification purposes only. Neither the author, photographers, publisher, nor this book are in any way affiliated with the manufacturers referenced in this book.

This is not an official publication from any of the dealerships mentioned in this book. The names of the dealerships are the property of the dealership. In the stories in this publication they are used for identification purposes only. Neither the author, photographers, publisher, nor this book are in any way affiliated with the dealerships referenced in this book.

Would you like to share a story in our next publication?
Send contributions to author@womenwhoridebook.com

ISBN-13: 978-0-9983303-4-1 (WiseWood, LLC)

Andreas, Sarah
True stories by, for, and about women with Rebel Souls, Golden Hearts and Iron Horses/Sarah Andreas
1.   Inspiration 2. Recreational 3. Self-Help

DEDICATION & ACKNOWLEDGMENTS

DEDICATION

To Dan and Marcus who are my two biggest supporters.
They often believe in me when I have doubts. I love their
sense of humor and love of life.

ACKNOWLEDGMENTS

To the women who ride and made this book possible.
This book is wonderful because of you!

CONTENTS

Foreword
Myra McElhaney

Do you know that there are approximately 1.2 million women who ride motorcycles?

Yep, 14% of the 9.2 million motorcycle riders are women according to the Motorcycle Industry Council's latest Motorcycle Owner survey. And our numbers are growing every day as more women are taking classes, buying bikes and riding.

I learned to ride and bought a bike at the ripe old age of 59. I'd ridden on the back with a guy in high school and loved it. Many years later, when I met the man who would become my husband I was happy to learn that he had a bike. I loved riding as his passenger during our seventeen-year marriage. Sadly, he passed away in 2009 from a brain tumor.

Apparently, it's easier to learn to ride and buy a bike than to replace a good husband! And for me, learning to ride wasn't easy. You see, somehow, I grew up in the country without learning to drive a manual transmission car. That made learning to ride a motorcycle more challenging.

The first mistake I made was signing up to take a class in July. In the South. It was 90+ degrees that day. With the required long sleeves, helmet and gloves, plus my jeans tucked into my knee-high Harley-Davidson boots I was dripping with sweat! One of the men in the class passed out from heat exhaustion and had to be taken away in an ambulance. It was that hot!

I wasn't prepared for how terrified I felt. I loved the sound and the feel of being on a bike again, but I was keenly aware of how dangerous it could be if I accidentally rolled the throttle too much. My bike kept going dead as I tried to start it. (I should have learned to drive a stick-shift car as a teen when my sister tried to teach me!)

After a few tries, the instructor, who was an older, tough-talking ex-military guy, became belligerent. He signaled for me to pull to the side. He straddled the front tire, held onto the handlebars, put his face just a few inches from mine and started yelling that I was "popping the clutch!" I didn't even know what that meant. I don't give up easily, but one thing I don't tolerate is being treated badly. His actions gave me crazy-abusive-controlling-first-serious-boyfriend flashbacks.

I said I was getting off the bike. He said I couldn't. I said, "Watch me!"

He said if I got off the bike he wouldn't let me back in the class. I got off and left.

I cried all the way home. I'd wanted to learn to ride a motorcycle so badly and had failed so miserably. And I was embarrassed. I'd told friends that I was taking the class, and they would ask how it went. And I'd have to say that I quit. I'm not a quitter, but I'd just quit something I really wanted to do.

Later, someone suggested that it may be easier to learn on a dirt bike. I took a dirt bike class. That instructor taught me how to listen to the bike and ease out the clutch. It was a lot of fun!

I took another Motorcycle Safety Foundation (MSF) street bike class. I failed! I still struggled with the clutch a bit and didn't do well enough on the maneuvers to pass the test. Oh, yeah, I wrecked the bike too! Still, I wasn't discouraged. I'd begun to calm my fear and enjoy the process.

The instructor, a nice guy who was committed to helping his students learn to ride, was sad to tell me I hadn't passed the licensing test.

"Hey, I don't own a bike," I told him, "so if I'd passed, I'd have to take another class to get my 'motorcycle fix.' Now I'll take another class to pass the license exam!"

Later, I took another class, passed the test and bought a bike. Then I took some one-on-one lessons to work on the slow maneuvers. Watching YouTube videos also helped me to understand how to coordinate the clutch and the throttle.

I share all this to say that if you're interested in learning to ride but are afraid, or if you've taken lessons and are still struggling to feel comfortable on your bike, keep at it! And you're not too old—I was 59 when I got my license! I thought that was late until I met a woman who got her license at 70! You can do it if your desire is strong enough! Any problems you have as you are learning are not failures unless you decide not to try again!

When I purchased my bike, the saleslady—that's right—sale lady (I like to support women anywhere I can!) gave me a few motorcycle magazines. Most had only ads and event listings, but one of the magazines, *Born to Ride Magazine*, included articles about people who ride.

Since I'm a writer and only a beginning rider, I pitched my dear friend, June Cline, "The Southern Sassy and Savvy Harley Riding Humorist" to be featured in an article. By the time the publisher and I got off the phone, I was a contributing writer with a column about women who ride! Isn't it cool when things you love come together?

June wrote the forward for Sarah's *Women Who Ride: Rebel Souls, Golden Hearts, and Iron Horses* book and introduced me to her as she knew Sarah would be a good fit for my column in *Born to Ride Magazine.*

Sarah's story of riding, working in the motorcycle industry, and her book about *Women Who Ride* made for an inspiring article. She and I have so much in common with our career backgrounds and interests in speaking, writing, riding and supporting women. I was delighted when she asked me to write the forward for this book.

So now you know a little about how I came to introduce you to Sarah's second book in the series, *Women Who Ride: Loving Life, Handlebars and Myself.* Here's what you'll find— stories of many amazing women who ride. (Kinda like the title says, huh?) As you read the essays from women of all ages, skill levels and walks of life you'll also find encouragement, humor and inspiration. Plus, you'll feel welcomed into this sisterhood of women who ride.

Now, find a comfortable spot, get a glass of something cold (or a cuppa something hot), put your feet up, and spend a little time with the stories of *Women Who Ride: Loving Life, Handlebars and Myself!* You're guaranteed to be ready to T-clock your bike and hit the road the minute you put the book down!

Enjoy life and do good!

Myra McElhaney
www.MyraMcElhaney.com

Myra is a writer and speaker who helps people to "Enjoy Life and Do Good!".

With over 20 years' experience giving keynote speeches, corporate training and writing, Myra is the author of Mama Always Says… and Musings on Major and Minor Matters that May or May not Matter and co-author of The Sun Sisters Guide to the Girlfriends Perfect Beach Vacation. Her memoir, Building A Life You Love After Losing the Love of Your Life was released in January 2016.

When not writing or speaking, Myra's active in her community through various non-profit organizations and participates in fundraising events for brain tumor research. For fun, she enjoys travel, entertaining and driving her red convertible in the North Georgia Mountains with the top down, the radio blasting and her hair blowing in the wind!

Chapter One – Sarah Andreas

"Just imagine what our world would be like if we encouraged all people to love life, to ride, and to embrace their journey, no matter their age or gender."

Sarah Andreas

fter I published the first *Women Who Ride* book I knew I had to do a second. The women who shared their stories were amazing, and they inspired others to share as well.

In the first book I shared that learning to ride helped me find a community of amazing people, both men and women. Here's an excerpt from my first book:

> People from all walks of life, from all passions and different experiences, [are] sharing their love of motorcycling. They have this beautiful camaraderie that is hard to find anywhere else. They come together to ride and nothing matters about their personal lives except the fact that they ride. The grandma, businesswoman, housewife, political parties, makeup or no makeup...the dividing lines seem to melt away in the presence of their love for the sport of motorcycling.

This book just as the first one is dedicated to all the women who have taken their passion for riding and turned it into a beautiful relationship with their motorcycles and the other women who ride. Riding seems to bring us the balance that we need in our lives. It brings peace, satisfaction and a sense of accomplishment.

Over the past thirteen years I have seen women who ride donate generously of their time and money to support great causes while riding. I have seen a woman stop what she was doing to help encourage a new rider to pick her bike up and get back on. I have experienced the women rider's willingness to share their "been there, done that" stories and encourage the woman who dropped her bike to have the determination to get back on and ride. I have also seen women riders have the courage to stand up for what they believe is right, and to hold their own against the family, friends and acquaintances who try to discourage them from riding a motorcycle.

Their love for riding is what makes this such a fun project.

When I put together the first *Women Who Ride* book I wanted to inspire future riders. I loved the stories and the connections that the book created, not just for me but also for the women who were a part of it. So, when I put out the call for contributors for this second book I was awed when Leilani Rosenbaum ask me if her two grand-daughters, who had started riding when they were little, could submit their story. Leilani says, "Girls who ride thrive," and I could not agree more. So, I said "Absolutely!" and Megan Grace and Karen each wrote short stories that are included next. I love that they are empowered to ride. *Now, I am pleased to introduce Karen.*

Karen

Hi, Mrs. Sarah, this is Leilani's granddaughter Karen with my story for your book. Hope you enjoy☐.

My name is Karen Bazor, and I'm 13 years old. I started riding on a go-cart when I was 6. Then I moved up to a PW 50 when I was 7 and a TTR 110 when I turned 10. I now have a TTR 125 (The Blue Thunder) and a Sherco trials bike (The Tiger Swallow Tail).

A few months ago, maybe in October, I went to ride at my grandparent's Extremophile Motor Cross track. It was not the first time I've been there on my 125. With my little sister close behind on her 110, we went zipping around like little speed demons with no boundaries. We came up to one of my favorite jumps and I decided to let her rip. I went over and caught some sick air, barely having time to take it all in. When I landed, my wheel was straight, and I had a grin on my face. I'll never forget how time stopped for me that day.

I don't think I could've ever made that jump without my greatest mentors, my grandparents. They're the ones who taught me everything I know and how to be confident when I ride. I still can't imagine where I'd be without them.

My dream is to one day become a world-renowned chef. I thank God for my wonderful talents in cooking, music, riding, and inspiring others. I love my piano, ukuleles, cat, and guinea pig. I want to make my guinea pig a mini-bike, but I haven't had the chance.

I love my family, Jesus, and riding. Riding has taught me how to be confident, courageous, and disciplined. I wish all riders luck and encourage them to do their very best. Karen B.

And now, let's hear from Megan Grace.

Megan Grace

Hi, Mrs. Sarah, this is Leilani's granddaughter Megan with my story for your book. My name is Megan, and I'm 11 years old. I started riding when I was 6. I remember the first time I caught sick air, I accidentally laid my hand on the throttle, so I flew over the jump. I was really scared when I landed. My first ride was also my first wreck. I was on my PW 50 when I made a sharp turn, flew into the bushes, and climbed a tree. I fell and started crying, so my dad came and pulled me out of the bushes. Other than that, I really don't have a favorite ride.

My very first, brand new bike came from Cycle Shack in Picayune, Mississippi. I got all new gear and was happy to have new stuff. It's my favorite bike because it's louder, sounds scarier, and it's faster. I call it The Blue Lighting, and it's a Yamaha TTR 110.

My grandparents taught me how to ride. I love animals, but dogs are my favorite. I want to open a dog boarding business when I grow up. I love my dog; her name is Pennie, and she's my best friend. I also have a guinea pig named Dumplin, he is a non-self tortoiseshell shorthair breed. He also has a big ego, so I put a mirror in his cage so he can look at himself. He and my sister's guinea pig share a cage.

After I ride, I take a shower, eat a snack, and have a dance party with my sister. One time, a hummingbird moth chased me around after I was done riding, so I screamed and ran around the yard 3 times. I am very happy to be in this book, and I wish the best of luck for all riders out there!!!

GIRLS WHO RIDE THRIVE!!!

Megan B.

Just imagine what our world would be like if we encouraged all people to love life, to ride, and to embrace their journey, no matter their age or gender.

Chapter Two – Leilani Rosenbaum

*"There is nothing a barapp of the throttle can't change—
with just a twist of the throttle!"*

Leilani Rosenbaum

THE BEST RIDE OF MY LIFETIME!

L ate January, my girls came and spent the night so that we could ride. The next day it took me seven hours to complete farm chores and dreaded office work. Megan patiently waited, because I promised to take her for a woods ride. Karen was going to ride her 125 Sherco for the second time and stay at the top of the property where M.T. could keep an eye on her.

So, I finally suited up and I was going to take Karen's 125TR so that Megan and I were on the same wheels, so to speak, as my 150CRF is not conducive to getting on or off if she needed help, and my 300 Montesa just wouldn't to give us the same experience of riding together.

Megan, of course, didn't want to wear the MX pants as they fit weird. I told her "No pants, no ride." She dutifully put them on. Megan informed me that because she waited all day I owed her a long ride through the enchanted forest of Shroomdom. So, I asked Tony to clip my phone on my back in case we want to stop and take a picture after I first videoed Karen as she rode around.

And off Megan and I went. We were having a great time. Paths were wet, some are flooded, so I went over proper body position and of course took the time to explain how important her MX pants are as the steam just rolls off the bike, and how she could have to make a trip to the Emergency room if she steamed her legs.

We came up on a really tough pass even when it's dry, the very first place I went down on, in 2010, on my first ride on my CRF 150 through the enchanted forest floor. A root lay crossways in the two-and-a-half-foot drop.

"Dang!" I went down, drenched, and it was January, so it was cold in South Mississippi that day. The bike is heavy when it's laying down, and I had to get wet again to get under it, pick it up, and then it started! I ran beside it as I walked it out.

I wanted Megan to help me, but when I asked for help she said "I can't. I'm stuck!" Yep, right behind me, she had no leverage to get off and drop her kickstand. I went to the other side to tell her to get on her bike and ride straight to me, reminded her of the root and not to cross it. But, no way. Down she went. Oh dang, now her little bike was down. Meg is ok. Mad, of course, telling me "I'm never riding again!" She was really wet, cold and scared.

I got her bike up. Yep, it started. Got to love these Yamahas. Tough little bikes! I've never ridden her bike because it's too small. So I was like, "What gear were you in?"

"I don't know."

"How do you shift into first gear?"

"Up," she said, "I think."

Ok. I got her bike to the other side. By then she was giggling and telling me "This is cool." And it was, in more than one way or another, literally COOL!

So, we got on, finished the rest of our ride in the woods, but decided to skip the track as were both shivering, just having a good ol' day on our steel ponies.

We went up to the top of the property searching for Karen. We found her down beside the pines, and what did I see but Karen balancing and riding flags that M.T. had put out for her to practice, going slow and balancing perfectly. This was the second time, mind you, on her Trials bike, a 125 Sherco she received early for her 13th birthday (which isn't until February 13th). I was like, "Let me grab my phone off my back." She was all smiles as she came by. I was like "Wow, look at you! Tell Mr. Ryan hi."

She came by. "HI!"

I was like, "Do you know how proud Mr. Ryan is going to be to know how well you're doing?" Ryan Young is a 6-time national trials rider, a Sherco and Scorpa dealer, and we will host him for a class here in South Mississippi in October for The Girls Who Ride THRIVE program! Ryan Young of RYP is an extortionary rider and a gifted teacher for all ages and experience (or none) on a trial bike, a true experience!

This same week was the week that I officially became a Sherco Scorpa dealer in South Mississippi to help the sport along. I love all my dirt bikes; they all serve a different type of riding.

So this will always remain my most favorite ride. The greatest part of all was that Megan went down and got back on. Karen is already showing the right attitude towards mastering a trials bike.

The coolest thing was that at the very beginning, unbeknownst to any of us, when Tony placed my phone on my back in its case he put the video recorder on. It was facing Megan as she rode behind me, so we have 18 minutes of our ride through the enchanted forest including both of us going down, the phone going underwater, and me using explicit language as I had to heave the bikes up and restart them. And Megan correcting Mia's, um, *frustrated language*, nothing a *barapp* of the throttle can't change with just a twist of the throttle! Just an unbelievable day to ride with my girls in South Mississippi!

Each year Karen and Megan will choose who The Girls who Ride THRIVE program will make a donation to.

Sarah Andreas' first book was the inspiration for our Girls Club, as Karen last year asked me, "Mia, what's the purpose of starting a club if we don't have a greater purpose?"

So I asked her, "Like, well ,what is your purpose for being a member?"

She said, "To spread the love of Jesus Christ."

So, we are girl by girl, the 3 b's—brains, brawn and beauty. Inner beauty, less it is fleeting! Nothing is more beautiful in life than being a part of helping God's great mission of changing lives one by one.

Our first donation is going towards Teen Challenge Women's Home here in Poplarville, Mississippi!

—Mia Mia, Karen and Megan's abundantly blessed, crazy grandma, as I'm known as! (Leilani Rosenbaum)

And now, here's a second story from Leilani. – Sarah

MY MOST PAINFUL RIDE

O n August 28th I decided to jump on my 300 Montesa Trials Bike. I named it Javelina. Javelinas are an indigenous American mammal that resemble pigs. They live in the forest and are known to occasionally BITE, if cornered. Yep! Appropriately named, I would say! He bites. And he bit me bad.

I planned to ride Javelina for the second time to get used to him by cruising the floor of our enchanted forest at Shroomdom, then take it all the way to the top of our property to the dirt track.

Before I took off, Tony said, "Hey, stop! We need to do a proper bike set-up."

I was like, "Come on, I'm already on and ready to go. You go ride, and when I come in from my ride, we can do it then." HUGE mistake. 100% RIDER ERROR. Or as

Mickey Diamond would say, "That was stupid really STUPID!"

Yep, as I finished an awesome ride, just a half of a mile from the shop, I went to jump a little bunny hop and the wheel locked to the left on a downward slope in fourth gear. I bit it bad. I hung on but couldn't reach the clutch lever, brake lever, or foot brake. And you guessed it—the throttle was still TWISTED WIDE OPEN in FOURTH GEAR!

So off I flew over my handlebar, onto my helmet, and slid over gravel, sticks and the Mississippi red dirt, which is DRY as a bone. That time of year, that dirt is hard as cement! I slid on a stick the last time I bush-hogged, and it entered my arm above my wrist and puncturing my arm up to my elbow. I also SLAMMED my hip and neck bad. I got up, shook it off, looked at myself, and blood was SPEWING from my arm when I moved it, just spewing out all over the dirt, my gear, and the rocks.

I was like, "Heck with that stupid bike!" even though, just before, I was riding through the woods enjoying my (then) most favorite bike.

So, I walked home. Tony came out and saw me crying and throwing my arms up. I told him, "Get the car! I need to go to the emergency room!"

Tony walked up cool, calm and collected, like a jarhead, and he had the audacity to say, "Come on. Come sit down on the porch and tell me what happened."

I was like, "WHAT! You get the phone and call Keisha!"

I called and told her, "Come and get me right now, I need to go to the emergency room." When Tony came out with ice packs I was out of my gear, and he looked at my hands. They were completely swollen, black and blue.

So, he was like, "Yeah, let's go!"

My eldest son was home visiting and staying with our neighbors. We called and asked them to come and pick up my bike.

So off we went to the emergency room, 45 minutes with me moaning and crying in severe pain. Poor Keisha and Tony. I guess I'm tough until I'm hurt or sick. Then I just want my Daddy, who has unfortunately passed. I will save you the embarrassing details of being admitted to the trauma center, especially since they might incriminate me. Let's just say that after being given the morphine, I did some serious interrogating of the trauma doctor whose luck it was to be working that evening.

After eight weeks of recovery and getting my sutures out, I asked my doctor, "Can I ride today?"

And the smart man that he is, he said, "Of course you can."

I also asked him to please write that on my release form so that I didn't have to fight with my family about riding so soon.

I showed Tony the note and asked him to please get Javelina out and start him, as I didn't think my arm and hands could handle it. Off to the top of the property, to the scene of the accident I went, and what happened? I turned around and ran out of FUEL. What a set-up! I walked home dejected. But I realized on the way that God knows better than stubborn, bull-headed prideful me.

Dr. Donaldson was a smart man. The day he took the sutures out he spoke with Karen and Megan about how important gear was. He told them that if Mia Mia hadn't been entirely suited up, how much worse my injuries would have been. Yep! MY GEAR TOOK THE HIT!

Funny thing was, that day I was walking over to the shed. I turned around, took my helmet off, went back into the gear locker and put on my chest protector. It must have been divine intervention, because I don't know how bad off I would have been sliding on my spine without it. Most trials riders don't wear them, but I do because I ride in our woods all the time and I've flipped off my MX bike, gone head over heels, and been lucky enough to stand straight up with no injuries. That's why gear is so essential. But I also love my bikes, all seven of them! Girls Who Ride THRIVE.

Leilani aka Mia Mia is from Mississippi. She was born on the island of Oahu, Hawaii and she says she was a Navy brat! She is the mother of four children and the grandmother of two girls. She rides dirt bikes with them. Leilani says that her husband is an awesome man who has encouraged her in many ways. He even helped her to become a certified Mississippi Volunteer Fire Fighter and First Responder. She is also a Certified Diver, both nitrox and advanced. Tony and Leilani learned to snow ski in their late 40's. Leilani is also proud that she is a certified heavy equipment operator. She says, "Tony made my lifetime dream come true. I'm a FARMER!" They built their farm together in Mississippi. They do field to forest farming, harvesting wild edibles from the forest floor, cultivating gourmet mushrooms and keeping bees in AZ hives from Slovenia. They practice conservation stewardship at all times wherever they are. She says that their rest and relaxation is riding dirt bikes and at times she is eating it!

You can email Leilani at Shroomdom38@outlook.com

Chapter Three – Amanda Gregory

"Every time I heard or saw a bike my head would turn, and my heart would skip with adulation."

Amanda Gregory

GET ON A BIKE AND FEEL
THE FREEDOM AND EMPOWERMENT

My first taste of motorbikes was when I was a young teenager. Even though I was born in Liverpool, at a very young age we moved to a small village in the county of Suffolk. Motorbikes were the local mode of transport, and I always admired them. My father, before he was married, used to road race, including the Isle of Man TT. I would spend hours looking at the old photographs. Not old enough to ride legally, I was always pillion traveling about with friends. I did get the opportunity to ride on private land, which is where I learned. It was always my intention to have my first bike as soon as I was old enough.

Unfortunately, life took a different turn, first with the loss of my father and then, a year later, my mother. I found myself transported back to Liverpool, and other things in my life took priority. Over the years I had very little contact with bikes but riding them always remained a dream. I never lost my passion for riding or bikes; every time I heard or saw a bike my head would turn and my heart would skip with adulation.

Despite those circumstances I went to university, where I earned my bachelor's in engineering, followed by several different jobs until I worked as cabin crew for British Airways and then had the opportunity to work in product research and development. Both those jobs I loved.

But I wanted to explore the world. This led me to my first visit to Nepal, where I remained for several years heavily involved in white rapid rafting, which is still a passion today, before returning to the UK.

On many fronts, I struggled in the UK, until in my late forties. I found myself jobless, destitute and practically homeless, and decided things had to drastically change. I was in the latter part of my life and had nothing to show for it. I decided to get qualified as a teacher, teach English as a foreign language, and travel again.

Within weeks of qualifying I landed a job in Indonesia. I spent 6 months in Jakarta before moving to another position in Jogjakarta. This turned out to be bike heaven and an opportunity for me to reacquaint myself with bikes and my love for riding. As Jogjakarta is a university city, it has a higher percentage of bike users than the average Asian city and is cheap to live in. Even though everyone was telling me that I must be crazy to want to ride there I wasn't deterred. I just wanted to have a bike and ride, so I did. By that time I was teaching in a school, and a very dear friend was teaching very close to me, so we both bought bikes enjoying the freedom of roaming around the city and taking off to the beautiful beaches. Riding through and around Jogjakarta city was a great training ground for learning control and maneuvering. Bikes are wheel-to-wheel and riders' are elbow-to-elbow; you need to be quick thinking and confident of getting around the city roads, but once I got into the mindset of how they ride there it became easy.

The earthquake of 2015 bought me back to Nepal as a volunteer, which is where I remain today. Here they have a different type of riding, with very windy roads, high mountain passes, and a variety of riding surfaces that here are classed as roads not to mention water often tumbling down the mountains across the roads and back down the mountains again. Being back in Nepal, which has always been close to my heart, has led me to where I am today. Not only am I riding these majestic mountain ranges, but living here has allowed me to turn my passion into a career by organizing adventure tours and tailoring tours for women. We also support environmental issues by donating to tree planting; one tree is planted for every rider who takes part. We stay in places that are mostly away from the tourist hotspots to generate income in low economic areas.

I wanted to encourage the women here to get on a bike and feel the freedom and empowerment it brings combined with the enjoyment of sisterhood. This led me to band together with two other riders to form the Himalayan Gypsies, the first women's bike chapter here. I am delighted that I am in a position to inspire and encourage women to ride in Nepal. We are part of the international organization Women in the Wind. The organization has been outstanding with their support, sponsoring women here by paying their membership fees so they can enjoy the benefit of being with such an international organization.

As our small band of women is growing, we can also reach

out to other women in remote areas. Being able to ride can play a very productive part in their lives. Nepal is a very patriarchal country and opportunities for women have been limited in the past, but times are rapidly changing.

I now have two training bikes to teach women riders in a safe and comfortable environment; it's not only about teaching them how to ride but also road safety and road awareness. The motorcycle test in Nepal teaches you how to control a bike but not much else. There is also virtually no safety riding gear for women, so I have teamed up with a beautiful couple from Delhi, Anjali and her husband Asish, who have recently designed a range of quality bike clothes for ladies.

My latest project is the Women Ride World Relay, a historical event which kicks off in the UK in a matter of weeks. I have been asked to be the ambassador for Nepal, which I'm very proud and honored to do. The relay will be passing through Nepal in July for 5 days, meeting the Indian contingent at the border and taking a route through Nepal to the Bangladesh border. The baton will be carried by a different woman each day, who will have with guardians with them all the way. This event is hugely encouraging to the women of Nepal, and it also challenging as it will take place in the height of monsoon season.

I am truly blessed that I can follow my dreams and passion. Dreams do come true if you keep dreaming and believing. Never doubt yourself and listen to your heart; the naysayers will fall by the wayside. The people around me sometimes think I'm a little crazy with my ideas but they always go along with me, and again I'm very blessed by this.

Amanda studied Combined Engineering Coventry University. She has worked in many disciplines connected to travel and hospitality, main employer British Airways, which she loved with a passion. In 2003 Amanda moved to Nepal and worked in White Rapid Rafting company before moving back to United Kingdom in 2005. In 2013 she moved to Indonesia to work as a teacher. Then in 2015 moved back to Nepal. Since moving to Nepal Amanda has set up the first ladies bike chapter WTTW Himalayan Gypsies.

Amanda has just stared her own motorbike tour company Wondering Spirits. https://www.facebook.com/adventuresofwonderingspirits/

Instagram adventuresofwonderingspirits

For booking tours http://freedomadventuretreks.com Wondering Spirits focuses on taking the roads less traveled, staying in low economic areas to generate income in to poor communities and being involved in environmental projects.

Chapter Four – Anastasia Turchetta

"She helped me nurture my self-confidence...stretch my limits...to be resilient when I fall... and to be proactive in my journey. Sometimes, the ride itself is...success."

Anastasia Turchetta

KICK START LIVING PASSIONATELY

A single photo exists of my grandfather riding his Harley with his youngest son in the sidecar. Family legend has it that my grandparents indulged in many adventurous rides from their rural coal mining town in PA all over the country.

Interestingly enough, however, not one woman in my family or inner circle of girlfriends has ever yearned to learn how to ride a motorcycle themselves.

Until me.

Originally, I was happy riding as a passenger. The problem was, I wanted to ride more often. And one day, asking to go for a ride lost its luster.

As you might imagine, that day triggered a healthy dose of self-reflection in my life. What would it be like to not have to ask? How would it feel to take the wheel of my own bike? And if that's what I truly wanted, what was the solution?

I needed to kick my asking to the curb. I wanted to stop riding through life passively. I deserved to own the cage-free life I'd dreamt of.

So, at age 45, I went for it. I studied. I passed. And I purchased my first ride off of eBay! Khalesi—my beautiful black and white 2009 Softail deluxe.

When Khalesi and I first met, we had to spend some quality parking lot time together. She had to know I was new at this; I had to learn that even though she was keyless, her fob had to be on my person to get her going.

Seems obvious, I know...

Imagine. It was a gorgeous Sunday, and I couldn't wait to show my off Khalesi to my in-laws and family. In all my excitement, I may or may not have forgotten my fob in my jacket inside. As we all walked out to the driveway, I proudly stood beside her. I confidently flipped the ignition. I was ready to hear her pipes roar.

Instead, I could hear a pin drop.

Twenty minutes of googling and a lot of awkward silence later, of all people, my mother-in-law asked, "Does she have a fob like a car?"

For the record, I have not made that mistake again.

Riding creates life experiences that are unmatched by planes, trains or automobiles. I found myself more involved in my community. I found myself getting more creative. When a friend asked me to be a part of a 5k, I transformed an old school 5k walk by adding some new school, Harley Davidson flare. She brought an incredible group of dental pros to do their thing; I brought a pack of riders to do the same. It was amazing and united. We helped hundreds of kids get gifted with dental care until they turn 18. Sometimes in order to embrace the journey we have to unleash the power of asking to contribute a different way.

From there, it was another dental trip in Paso Robles, CA with CDA Cares. Cyclists got their exercise on; riders rode the foothills of California wine country. And yours truly? I learned.

I learned to ride even better. More importantly, I learned I wasn't alone. There were cage-free seekers everywhere. We just had to find each other.

In short, since Khalesi and I have teamed up, I have grown to overcome many fears. I've had to re-assess respect. I've had to give in to vulnerability. Vulnerable to weather conditions, road conditions, horrible drivers, flying objects out of the back of vehicles, animals, etc.

The old me would have chosen to take a detour. The new me wants to live my best life.

Khalesi has increased my self-confidence. She's taught me that each ride is an experience. She has helped me nurture my self-confidence...stretch my limits...to be resilient when I fall...and to be proactive on my journey.

Sometimes, the ride itself is success.

Sometimes, the success is being present. Our ability to disengage with technology and live in the moment with those we cherish is the win.

I'm thankful that the occasional ride was no longer good enough. My ride to success today is with work-life wellness. I chose to get my license to thrive. Will you?

Take what you learn and make a difference with it!

Anastasia, RDH is a health empowerment conversationalist whose voice of experience ignites your route to personal and professional health. A curiosity expert and coffee addict with 30 years in the healthcare profession, her programs share how to align your emotional, physical and financial health to lead a more productive life. Reduce daily stress, energize your profitability, take the wheel and pick a lane to thrive in it. See www.AnastasiaTurchetta.com

Chapter Five – Barb Goodrow

"I didn't realize, and many others may not, the importance of friendships, acquaintances, camaraderie, and the fellowship of like-minded women who have this deep-rooted desire to ride motorcycles."

Barb Goodrow

DO IT NOW AND DON'T HAVE REGRETS

As I sit down to write I'm at a loss for where to start. My goal is to encourage other women to ride and continue to grow and explore, and to lead by example. So much has changed in my life since I got back into riding motorcycles and yet a lot is the same.

First, I can say that my life has been greatly enriched and I feel very blessed. I think many women get to their middle age years—you know, the empty nest, menopausal years— and still haven't taken time for themselves and figured out what they truly want and need in the next chapter of life facing them. I was one of them.

When I purchased my first Harley, the salesman told me, "It's a whole new way of life." At the time I didn't know what he meant. But as I joined the local HOG chapter and began riding and meeting new people I started to understand. I had lived rather quietly, somewhat non-socially for many years. And I knew I was starved, but didn't realize how starved I was for conversation, things to look forward to, events to plan and save money for, and most of all that feeling of camaraderie and being part of "something." The biker world is huge and exciting! And I am passionate about it! Especially women who ride.

I didn't realize, and many others may not, the importance of friendships, acquaintances, camaraderie, and the fellowship of like-minded women who have this deep-rooted desire to ride motorcycles. It's funny, either you have it or you don't. So many times I've had older women, (I'm 60) and younger women also, wrinkle their noses and say they can't believe I'm riding a big motorcycle. They don't have it, and they just don't get it. I have such a desire to ride and see different places, feel the wind, smell my surroundings and just explore all the beauty! I love being adventurous. I don't take risks, but I don't sit still and let life pass by either.

When those who don't "get it" ask why I ride, I respond by telling them that in the past five years since I bought my first Harley I've met more wonderful people, made new friendships, traveled to more new exciting places, and done more fun things outside my comfort zone than I had in the past 25 years of my life! Honestly.

One of the greatest things has been participating in the yearly "Chick's ride" from Doerflers' Harley-Davidson, my local Harley-Davidson dealership. This ride is planned and led by one of the owners, Deanna Doerfler. Deanna started these rides 15 years ago, with the goal in mind of helping women in our area to become more independent and gain confidence with motorcycling, and to grow their market base of women and provide an opportunity to network and share their common interest of riding and creating friendships.

I've joined in on the past five yearly rides and have loved every one. This is a whole "family" in itself! Each year I've met new "chicks" and become better acquainted with ones met previously. Sometimes we won't see each other in person until the next year's ride but we may keep in touch throughout the year on social media.

We've all shared laughter, mostly, and group adventures. We share life stories, riding stories, relationship stories, and tears. There is usually at least one activity that all "chicks" are encouraged to attend such as river rafting, ziplining, riverboat dinner cruising, etc. This has all meant the world to me! I feel like I belong, at least for those few days. I've learned to tell the ladies that I love them and give many hugs, which was totally out of my comfort zone.

We come from all walks of life. There are teachers, daycare providers, business owners, healthcare providers, stay home moms...you name it, there's one among the chick riders. We don't cause trouble, we're not obnoxious. We just love life and have fun! It's really quite a sight when 30-40 women on motorcycles get together. The people we meet along the way and at our destinations usually really enjoy us. If I hadn't gone with the chick riders, I probably would never have seen some of these destinations and would have missed so much!

Another way my life has been enriched is through the couples my husband and I have met and ridden with. e may not see each other outside the motorcycle world but we really enjoy our time together when we ride. On one such occasion, while traveling through Columbus, Nebraska, as I was riding through town I approached a stop light. Two lanes over a lady in a nice SUV put her window down and pointed at me and yelled, "I want to be you"! I smiled and yelled back ,"DO IT!" My heart soared. Now this is living, even if it is 95 degrees with a 30 mph wind.

On another occasion, I was solo riding in the fall, and it was a beautiful leathered-up day. As I was cruising along a rural highway, I had to slow down and follow a pickup with a large round bale on the back. When it was clear to pass I could see the driver quickly cranking the old-style window down, and he raised his arm out the window and gave me a big "thumbs up" and a big smile.

My only regret is that I didn't "embrace the journey" and get back into riding many years ago. Ride safe ladies, do it now and don't have regrets!

Barb *contributed to* Women Who Ride: Rebel Souls, Golden Hearts, and Iron Horses. *She currently rides a 2016 Heritage.*

Chapter Six - Chris Keeble

"I inspire my kids and now grandkids into knowing that women can be fierce, strong, independent, caring, gentle and wonderful creatures."

Chris Keeble

IRON HORSE MUMMA

I've been riding for many years, stopped for many years to have a family, and now I'm watching my grandkids grow.

After my marriage ended a decade or so ago, I decided to get back in the saddle and feel that rush again. This bike is my fourth, and every bike I have, I love to spend time designing a look. Part of my creative bent, I guess. This will more than likely be my last motorbike that will see me reach 100! I love riding by myself and with friends. I don't like those big groups and too many people, so while I have joined them, I don't last long. Too many rules and too many instructions.

I guess I'm most proud of the fact that I inspire my kids and now grandkids into knowing that women can be fierce, strong, independent, caring, gentle and wonderful creatures. There are no rules except to be a good person. Being independent, different, open-minded and ready to experience the world and its people regardless of race or religion is a great attitude to have.

I will often be riding along and hear other drivers beeping me. It's a nuisance because I think something is wrong, but they get up next to me with their cameras, taking pictures or videos of me and the bike. Then I get a thumbs up and off they go. Stopping also creates a crowd around the bike. Whenever I see kids, I ask them if they would like to sit on it. Parents take a shot, and everyone's happy. I'm sure there are pics of the bike and random people and me all around the world.

I work hard and long hours, running a small business, working a full-time job, and helping with the grandkids, so any free time I have, it's a date with Calamity Jane. And don't we have fun!!

I have a saying—well I have a few, actually—but this is my main one: *tradition is the illusion of permanence.* I like to push the boundaries, do things differently and test normality and what people think it is. I think the buzz word now is "disrupters." That's me. In business and in professional life, I like to disrupt and always look to see if things can be done differently. I hate that saying, "If it ain't broke, don't fix it." I say, "if it ain't broke, try breaking it and rethinking it." Being creative and coming up with ideas in all areas of my life is so satisfying. I believe ideas' are the most important thing to have in business and in life. Without ideas and creative thought, we can never progress.

There is, at this stage of my life, no time for a relationship. Quite frankly, I'm happiest on my own, calling my own shots and spending time with family and mates when I choose. There is no shortage of possibilities!!! I just don't want to be looking after anyone else now. Time for me.

Time for me and Calamity Jane!

Here's another story from Chris.

"Well behaved women rarely make history"

Laurel Thatcher Ulrich

I WANT TO LIVE MY LEGACY

I started riding way back in my very early 20's. My husband at the time had a motorbike, and I really disliked being on a pillion. So, I decided that rather than miss out, I'd get my license and ride alongside him, not behind him. Something about that philosophy works for me to this day. Life is about working and walking alongside people, in all its forms!

My first bike was a little thing that was made of bits and pieces but was the legal size for a learner. It did me just enough and fell to bits virtually the week I became able to go up to larger size bikes. It was like it knew its time had come. Funny how bikes seem to have their own personality!

I then jumped on a Harley Davidson Sportster 883 Custom. That was such a great bike. I threw it around like a BMX. I thought for a moment I could be part of the Crusty Demons show (a touring motorbike show of stunt riders)! I was also a responsible mum...so settle down!

Like most motorbike riders, I started to get a bit of an addiction and wanted bigger, faster, fancier things. I then upgraded to several larger Harley-Davidson's for the next 30-plus years. I loved them all, and all were very different.

I'm a bit of a creative soul, and I tend to bespoke my bikes to within an inch of their lives. So, they become a talking point. I love seeing people admire the bikes and the work I've done to them. I always allow kids to sit on the bike, so mums and dads can take pics!

The past few years I've had a bit of a dream to own an Indian motorcycle. I'm not sure what it is about them, but I like the backstory and the look of them. However, I was intimidated at first with just how big they are—much bigger than anything I've ever ridden. After three years or so of wondering, I jumped on over and now ride a Chief Vintage Classic. It's a dream to ride. The more you ride, the better you become, and you are never too old to improve and learn. It's a big bike and has tested me at times with its power and handling in tight spots. I test rode many Indian motorbikes, and while I think there are a couple there that were more comfortable for me I went with the Vintage because I had a clear idea of what I wanted to create. Meet Calamity Jane. It's a showstopper and a talking point wherever we go. I LOVE her!

It seemed a natural thing for me to look at life and a transition to retirement, and I believe Calamity Jane and I will ride off and do great things together. She is my passport to travel, people, places and music. My other real passions are music and writing, producing shows, supporting artists and creative folk. I'm joining the dots with these two areas of my life. I enjoy riding by myself or with a small group of riders. I'm not one for those big groups and clubs.

I ride all over Australia and hopefully the world. I love riding in the US. It's like when they built the roads they were thinking of motorbike riders! The roads are in great condition there. Australia has a bit to learn with that. Some of the roads are death traps and shockers. I've had some seriously close calls that have made grown men pull over, go ashen white and wonder how I managed to stay upright!

However, there are some magical places still for me to discover in Australia. So much to do! I'm now 60 years old. Can't believe it and I feel I'm just getting started. I have more energy than when I was in my 30's!

I have two grown daughters and two beautiful granddaughters. I want to be a role model for them. I don't want to be pigeonholed into being an expectation to anyone. If you set your mind to it, you can make anything happen.

Someone said to me the other day, "Chris, you're a way finder." That made my day! I want to live my legacy, and I hope I can inspire and help others in all sorts of ways. Calamity Jane and myself...the two of us.

I have a couple of sayings. "There's a crack in everything, that's how the light gets in," There's a Leonard Cohen song that to this day helps me out when things don't always go to plan. Being a high achiever and a perfectionist at times, I need to learn to give myself some slack, and remember that everything always leads to something great. Some things just need to go wrong before you get to right!

The other saying is, "Well behaved women rarely make history." That's a quote from Eleanor Roosevelt. I love reading about women and how brave they are and the things they do. We are such special creatures. I love breaking down stereotypes, pushing the boundaries and being brave and crazy!

For any lady wanting to learn to ride, start with something small (even a scooter, for they are so much fun. I still have one, and I LOVE buzzing around on that too). However, it's not about size, really, it's about becoming road smart. Once you feel a connection with being so open and free. Then you can look at upgrades. Gain confidence with the road and the environment. Then go for it. Never say a bike is too big. It's not about size, it's all about technique. Learn, practice and watch videos. And always ride within your comfort zone and don't let anyone force you to be faster or take risks. I ride with a few very fast guys. I say, "Off you go, you show-offs. See you at the other end, have a drink waiting for me, please!" I'll take in the scenery and enjoy the moment. I don't need to be tearing it up around corners, etc.

I've developed a page called "The Aussie & The Indian" on Facebook, Instagram, and a YouTube channel. I blog, tell stories, meet people, review products, etc. If nothing else, my daughters and granddaughters will have that to look at in the future.

Life is so much fun. It's crazy busy, but fun! I make it my choice to wake up each morning with that attitude. And Calamity Jane always puts a smile on my face!

Thanks for reading. Ride safe and see you on the road sometime. X

Chris *is a writer, producer, promoter, living within the entertainment industry across all types of areas such as theatre, clubs, pubs, and corporate venues, to name a few.*

With a triple major BA degree in Theatre Theory and Practice, Marketing and Multi-Media, Chris has over the years produced many events from curating art exhibitions to rugby league matches, managed theatres and sat on industry boards.

Outside of her busy working life Chris spends most of her time with her grandchildren and riding her beloved Indian motorbike, Calamity Jane.

You can find her online at:
https://www.facebook.com/TheAussieandTheIndian/
https://www.instagram.com/theaussie_and_theindian/
https://www.youtube.com/channel/UC5IfGyP-z6-sVUxeQF4pmsw?&ab_channel=TheAussie%26TheIndian
or email chris@ckck.com.au. -

Chapter Seven – Deborah Grant

"Two sisters riding off into the wind celebrating their victories that they have earned."

Deb Grant

LIFE BEHIND BARS

I have been riding as long as I can remember. As a small girl, I wanted to grow up and do my own stunts like Steve McQueen did. From motocross to street bike riding, it has been a journey of a lifetime. So many great adventures with so many wonderful people.

In 2000, at 37, I decided to do hare scrambles, which is a form of motocross. I rode a Yamaha TTR125. I loved that bike! It was lightweight and easy to tear down after every race, and it fit me like a glove. I did that with my friend Paula (who raced quads) for three years, until I was catapulted off my bike at age 40. Laying in the ambulance, I decided it was better to quit while I could still walk.

In June of 2011, I was diagnosed with breast cancer. When I was diagnosed it changed my life forever. I wanted to tell my favorite aunt who lived up in New Hampshire, the bad news in person. It didn't hurt that in Laconia, the bike rally, was going on too. I rode north with my friend Linda, who was going to Vermont. When we hit the Bennington Exchange in Vermont we parted ways. Five miles down the road the sky got black and the wind started to blow. For 80 miles I rode in a hurricane until I got to Plymouth, New Hampshire. The wind was throwing me all over the road. There were times I had to remove my goggles because they were steamed up, and the rain was coming down so hard it was sideways. When I finally arrived, my hands were so numb my uncle had to take off my gloves.

One of my greatest memories that I hold close to my heart is about my sister Kathy and how she helped me get through my recovery from cancer. She has a medical background in chemotherapy. Her reaction rocked me to my core, she was so upset. Every day after work she would come over, and we would pass the time playing Scrabble.

One of my biggest fears was that I would never be able to ride again. I would go out and sit on my bike, and it was painful just to stretch over to grab the handlebars after my surgery. My sister would always assure me that I would ride again, but I had to give it time. We would talk about making a sister trip together some day.

My first surgery was in August, and my last in October, with three in total. The hospital where I had my surgeries had a charity event called Cyclefest, which was two weeks after my final operation. I participated in the ride even though I still had stitches. I met so many interesting people and had the time of my life. The very first rocker I ever got was from that event; you should see my vest now!

A few years after my recovery my sister was diagnosed with diabetes and skin cancer. I felt the weight of the world crashing down on me, one hurdle after another. We swore that if we got through this, we would make that sister trip together. I am happy to say she won the battle, and the destination of our three-day weekend trip was to Jim Thorpe, PA. We were two sisters riding off into the wind and celebrating the victories that we earned. We spent the weekend at a biker friendly B and B, hiking, riding, and bonding as we rode to the top of Bear Mountain to watch the sunrise.

That experience led me to believe that I could be an active part in helping other women obtain their goals by sharing my story and encouraging them to pursue their dreams in the face of adversity.

Through the years, I have participated in many worthy charity rides to help raise awareness for a variety of causes, including cancer. Last year I was asked to speak at the Mid-Atlantic Women's Motorcycle Rally.

As I carry on with my life behind bars, I reflect upon how something bad can turn into something great with the help of family and a 2015 Blue Honda Stateline. I hope one day my sister can join me at the rally. I know she would love the sisterhood of bikers as I do.

Deborah has been riding for 40 years. Starting at age 11 and riding a mini-bike, she knew then that riding would be her destiny. At the age of 15, she rode a Yamaha 100 with her sister Kathy on the back, flying through the soccer fields of Penny Pack Elementary School trying to outrun the police. She now works at Princeton University in New Jersey in the shipping and receiving department. Everyone knows her and her 2015 Royal Blue Honda Stateline as she rolls onto campus in her leather jacket.

Chapter Eight – Donna Poole

"My first thought was to get a motorcycle. And the giddy feeling I felt one second after that thought I will never forget."

Donna Poole

FIND THE SASSY KID AGAIN, BE WILD AND FREE

I'm always amazed at the women I meet who ride motorcycles. I didn't think I had a preconceived idea about what kind of woman rides, I'm a very open-minded person…but when I answered an ad for a biking vest on a website and met a retired bank executive at the blood donor clinic she was volunteering at, it made me smile so big.

My story is probably similar to many other women riders'. As a teenager, with my mother standing on our front step yelling that I would kill myself, I would jump on the back of my friend's bike and go for a rip on beautiful country roads. The thought of having my own bike never entered my mind. It just wasn't what girls did then.

Life happily carried on: university, work, marriage, children, and very reliable family cars and vans happened.

At 50 I found myself living alone, both kids in university, and myself with a new diagnosis of breast cancer. As I looked at all the possibilities and what ifs I thought to myself, "Wow, if I did die, would I have regrets? If I was told I had x number of months to live, what would I do with that time?" Hypothetically, I knew I would want to spend that time with family and close friends, but I also knew I would want to have a lot of fun. Find the sassy kid again, be wild and free.

That was the last time I thought about dying. I sat down

and said, "Ok, pick something fun that you want to do when this cancer treatment is done. Anything. Shit just got real. Nothing is off the table."

My first thought was to get a motorcycle. And the giddy feeling I felt one second after that thought, I will never forget. Like when I was a kid at Christmas. Pure fun. And that feeling returns every time my leg goes over my bike.

During radiation treatment, I bought my first motorcycle. Two weeks after treatment I passed my motorcycle course, and the rest, as they say, is history.

I love the happy feeling of being on my bike. It is freedom like no other. I can't explain it, really. I smile every time I get on my bike, truly.

I've been riding for four years, am on my third bike. I've ridden thousands of miles and look forward to riding thousands more. I've met wonderful people who ride. I've seen beautiful scenery I wouldn't otherwise have seen. I've seen so many bald eagles soaring when I ride. There is no roof on a bike, the sky is wide. Which brings me to inclement weather. Yes, you are at the mercy of the elements, sometimes it is wet and cold, but the camaraderie of a bunch of wet bikers is an experience shared. I pack a tent on my bike and go camping. I ride solo, or with biker friends, in group rides. All bring their own kind of fun.

I'm a nurse. Yes, I've taken care of patients surviving motorcycle accidents. I've also cared for patients as they died after living a safe and healthy life. Make your peace, live your life, enjoy every moment you can.

Donna *rides a 650 V Star. She describes herself as a daughter, sister, friend, nurse, mother, and a lover of life. She shares that she loves her bike, the freedom and the down to earth people she meets.*

Chapter Nine – June Cline

"There are no words to capture that moment. I was mainlining God. I was one with my soul. And I knew what pure grace, delight, and gratefulness felt like. And I still do, every time I ride."

June Cline

HANG ON!

P assion
"Hang on," he said after he had picked me up and plopped me on the back seat of his Harley-Davidson. Away we went —with a little fishtail in the back wheel on that gravel-dirt Virginia road—by the canal bank where my grandparents lived.

I was 10, terrified, excited and hooked!

Hanging on for dear life to the waist of my Momma's middle brother, Uncle James, oh, that ride was too short. But long enough to give birth to a lifelong feeling of freedom and longing. "I want me one of these!"

We had already made the turn back down that gravel road when I yelled over his shoulder and the loudness of those pipes, "Can we go again, Uncle James?" That's when we both saw her—Momma.

There she stood, in the very spot where Uncle James's Harley had been parked. Both hands were clenched in a firm fist on the waistline of her full-skirt dress, her stance about a foot wide, her jaw set in locked position with a look that said, "Both of you are gonna die." She was hotter than those pipes that Uncle James forgot to warn me about. DOUBLE OUCH!

Uncle James killed the motor, and I knew Momma was going to kill us. With the perfect amount of silence and glare, my first two names were her first words followed by, "If I EVER catch you on the back of a motorcycle again, I will beat you half to death. You can die on one of those things!" Momma's math and meaning were clear, and on that day, Uncle James and I were gonna get to live. But my future was iffy if ever again I was on two wheels.

Courage

So, of course, my first boyfriend had a motorcycle, which my Momma KNEW ABOUT, and I KNEW to NEVER be on the back of it. In fact, Momma's mantra to me always was, "I will trust you until you show me I can't." And, vividly seared in my brain was, "if I ever CATCH you on the back…"

So, clearly, the answer was around the corner from my house—where I would jump on the back of William's 750 Honda, and away we went on many great adventures: Lake Lurleen State Park, Holt Lock and Dam, Denny Chimes on the campus of The University of Alabama, in Tuscaloosa, AL, where I grew up. And just like with Uncle James, I would hang on tight with my arms around William's waist but yelling different words above his pipes. "One day, I'm gonna ride in front!"

Our biggest adventure—well, our closest call—was the day we pulled up to a red light next to a Ming Green Plymouth Fury, right beside my Momma in her car, which was appropriately named because hell would hath no fury like a Momma scorned! I flipped my face away from her, and yelled to William, "TURN RIGHT! TURN RIGHT!

WHEW! At 15, William and I barely missed the apocalyptic fury of Momma! But more importantly, I had barely missed the loss of her trust.

It would be a lifetime of Harley-Davidson tchotchke's, Christmas ornaments, t-shirts and gifts from well-meaning family and friends who knew I loved Harley's. Of course, none of that could quench my longing to "go again." What it would take was a divorce from a 22-year marriage (not to William), and a 1,953-mile move from Atlanta to Phoenix, AZ, before I dared to make those words come true—"One day, I'm gonna ride in front."

My very first "single" Sunday afternoon in AZ, I found myself at Hacienda Harley-Davidson in Scottsdale trying on Harley's. There was one, a deep maroon color Softail Deluxe, totally tricked out with fringed leather seat, saddlebags and chrome everywhere. It was so me! I had the money, but not the courage. I still regret leaving her there. But there were a million reasons to—like, I didn't know how to ride. And Momma.

Freedom

Two years later, a dear friend and I were in my car headed to a meeting in San Diego, where I would be speaking. She received a brief but serious family call on her cell phone, with lots of "oh no's, uh-huh's, I'm so sorry's," and "I understand". She abruptly turned to me, and with an attitude asked, "Do you want a Harley or not?"

WHAT? A family member of hers had to immediately sell her brand new 2005, 883 Custom Deluxe, Custom Low Sportster Harley-Davidson with 83 miles on the odometer. A Harley-Davidson literally fell in to my lap while driving my car to San Diego. Sight unseen, not knowing how to drive a motorcycle, nor if my feet would even touch the ground— which William and I had discovered in a parking lot at age 15—was extremely important. I said yes. Forty-five years after my first ever "hang on" freedom ride with Uncle James, I had my Harley.

The significance of my lifelong longing unfolding from the front seat of my car was astonishing. Nothing had changed in the two years since I sat on the seat of that beautiful maroon chromed out bike with my heart pounding and my feet firmly on the ground and her begging me to buy her, and I said no. But in my car that day, I said yes to my longing because someone else was in trouble. Someone else needed help, and my helping her would give me what I wanted—the courage to give myself permission to "ride in front." How often had I done that—said "No"—to me?

Suddenly, I was in a class learning to "ride in front," and THAT was a steel horse of a different color. I was terrible at it, terrified, and with classmates who secretly named me most likely NOT to succeed. I would fall over for no reason. In fact, I flunked my class because I dropped the course bike in the dreaded figure eight box. Game over. But I was allowed to come back the next day and retake the figure eight driving test, and I passed. This did not give me comfort as I was still terrified and still dropping my bike, which I affectionately named "Good Golly Miss Molly." Six months and two additional instructors later, I was finally "road ready."

Michael, my fav instructor, cared enough to take a small group of his four ridding misfits out on the road. It was my Uncle James' magical memory-making moment on steroids and is forever etched in my soul. *I was riding in front!* Still terrified and THRILLED, I was following Michael headed north on, yes—Power Road!

Leaving neighborhoods and civilization behind, we rounded a curve and there it was, an "Oh My God," panoramic view of a stunningly beautiful desert, glorious mountains in the distance, with three-armed cactus sprinkled roadside and all across the valley of Tonto National Forest. I spontaneously let out an scream at the top of my lungs for as long as my air lasted– "THANK YOU GODDDDDDD!!!!" There are no words to capture that moment. I was mainlining God. I was one with my soul. And I knew what pure grace, delight, and gratefulness felt like. And I still do, every time I ride.

Something else I learned that day–it's not good to cry on a motorcycle at 50 miles an hour. And, blowing or wiping your nose and tears in a full faced helmet, well, it's just not doable.

It took me a year to tell my Momma, and I can tell you that at age 54 I was still terrified. Ironically, sitting at a red light in her car, a group of about 30 bikers were passing in front of us. It was time.

"You know Mom, I finally broke down and bought me one of those."

Her response was, "I HEARD!"–in that same tone I'd heard at 10—of "If I EVER..." The silence was deafening and long. Then, I heard my Momma say, "Well, you'd better take care of my little girl."

"I will, Momma," I replied. But in my head, heart and soul, I said only to me, *I did Momma. I hung on to my dream, and it fell in to my lap, and I said yes, and I get to ride in front and go again and again.*

Later that night, I told her the story of William and me and her at the red light. She looked at me with a love and conviction that fuels my soul to this very day and said, "June, I could've looked straight at you, and I would not have seen you because I trusted you so much." Sometimes there are no words for a mother's love.

Thank you, God, thank you, Uncle James, for my motorcycle passion, confidence, and freedom. And Momma, thank you. I am so grateful and blessed that I always had your unconditional love, caring, and trust — even on two wheels. I KNOW you watch over Miss Molly and me now, Momma. I love you, and I miss you – still.

June is *President of the Center for Laughing and Learning and Creator of the B.R.A.S.S. Bra Woman Online Mentoring Program, June Cline is a keynote speaker, author and entrepreneur. June has performed on stage at convention centers across the country and Canada, as well as in well-known comedy clubs like Rick's House of Comedy in Phoenix, AZ and The Punchline in Atlanta, GA. When she's not making people laugh and learn, you can find her riding her Harley, Good Golly Ms. Molly, on the beautiful twisty back roads of North Georgia. She loves coming home to Kennesaw, Georgia and her "mens" as she calls them, the light-of-her-life, Jerry Cline, and the Lucky Man, their rescued "crazed"` Shih Tzu. Together, the three of them "Make Life a Great Ride." Connect with June at JuneCline.com and on Facebook, LinkedIn, and Twitter.*

Chapter Ten – Laurie Ann Leach

"We all have a path of our own, and my bike, "Lil Girl," certainly knows how to find our way on it, I am just a willing participant."

Laurie Ann Leach

LOVING GOD, LIFE, AND MOTORCYCLES

I t's a beautiful day, the sun is shining, I feel good, and no-one's gonna stop me now… oh yeah, it's a beautiful day, I feel good, I feel right, and no-one, no-one's gonna stop me now…it's hopeless to even try," by Queen, is at high volume on my Bose system in the house, perfectly invigorating. The piano is crystal clear and beautiful. I hope my neighbors like it, teehee! I 'Mitting on my front step, sipping my hot morning tea, watching the sunrise, readying for my adventure at hand and waking the neighbors with my morning inspiration. Good thing they like me! They'll be awake soon anyways when I crack the throttle on my bike to leave!

It's another glorious sun-filled morning, and life contemplations run through my mind like a passenger train, flipping from one scene after another as if looking out the window as the countryside and sights fly by. I hear another bike off in the distance, jolting me back to reality. I am not the only one with these thoughts of Wind Therapy! I am excited for today, the first day in my new adventure, ready to connect more fully with the Holy Spirit who is directing me into a new life worth living that nurtures my spirit and soul, and for which I've prayed daily.

It's been a tough road. I've made my share of mistakes: with my boys, as does any parent (love them more than life itself, but I'm not perfect); in love, FOR SURE; finances— yes, well, um—; friendships, ahem; and trust, wow, yeah; all causing me illness and untold physical pain. But now I know the error of my ways and have certainly learned from the Lord's boot to my butt. Thinking about the past has been counterproductive and has kept me stuck in the mire of old news.

It was time to create new headlines and find the meanings of happiness and joy for myself, instead of working on fixing that for others. We all have a path of our own, and my bike, "Lil Girl," certainly knows how to find our way on it. I am just a willing participant.

Let me tell you about a favorite trip. The sun was rising, and the beauty of the day ahead had become very apparent. Oranges and yellows were coating everything and the sun felt so warm on my face and my leathers. At 60 degrees, clear and sunny, it was an idyllic morning. Lil Girl was all packed up and waiting in the driveway in front of me, where I had rolled her out before the dawn. Shiny clean, full tank, tires and oil checked, and all my gear was stowed, carefully balanced and secured. She was ready and so was I. I'd delayed this trip long enough, getting my house in order, now it was time to roll.

I'd spent the last few months mapping out the things I wanted to see in a triangle from east North Carolina (where I live) to Georgia's Oconee National Forest. From there up through the Chattahoochee and Nantahala National Forests, spending time scooting around, so many great roads here and some of the most beautiful rides I've ever experienced with sharp dives and perfectly banked curves, and across on obscure routes like Route 64 and 23 with its over 12 sets of waterfalls and War Woman Road in Clayton (with a stop at Dairy Queen to celebrate at the end).

They say, "She's bipolar—completely different going one way or back." I agree.

Route 276 to Cedar Mountain and Mountain Bridge, Route 180 to Brasstown Bald lookout, the highest peak in Georgia, has views of four states. I spent an evening or so in the world-famous Austrian town of Helen. After some great food and tchotchke shopping, I headed towards Asheville for some sightseeing, then on to Spartanburg, heading home on Route 211, which took me around the city and crisscrossing on wandering roads.

The riding was thrilling in the shades of green with the sun peeking through and strobing in time with my speed. The smells continually changed in the areas I swooped through, down into the pasture lands and up into the mountains where the vistas are truly God's creation for our enter-tainment. It heals me on so many levels it is difficult to describe them all, but opening my heart center to move my life along and forward is probably the most fascinating and soul-stirring of them all. The absolute thrill of freedom is better than any drug on the market and opens my mind to new possibilities. I'm a prisoner no more.

Three weeks gave me time to see some of God's beauty as I was riding through, and the quaint little towns sprinkled throughout that I have found so welcoming. I had goosebumps, crawl bumps, or goose pimples, as some people call them. Here in the south, they say its confirmation from the angels that you are on the right path. I sincerely hope that it is the truth. But I was thoroughly excited anyways.

I've made trips alone before, but not for so long, and not in such remote areas; yet, I was not afraid. I feel these trips, especially for women, are so clearing for our psyche. They're a time to reflect on and to take care of only ourselves, a time for us to do and see exactly what we would like to do and see and take our time to do it. A time to think about what we want our lives to look like, and if we want do it alone or with a partner that truly understands us as the Warrior Women we are. We are stronger than we have ever been, smarter and more intuitive. It takes a different kind of partner now to understand and appreciate us.

Going into nature helps us find ourselves. Connecting with God, whoever that is for you, and speaking with Him/Her, asking for guidance and assurance is easier when we are in the quiet. I find these areas without electronic disruption help to quiet the noise and the static of daily life and let the flow happen in peace. And when I say these areas are remote, I mean it. There are some areas where there is no cell service or GPS, so be sure to map out your route on paper and keep it handy—truly, getting back to basics.

So, my Sisters, Love Goddesses, Warriors, Princesses, Queens, and Bitches, come with me on two wheels or three, the best is yet to be. Let's live life while we are full of it and allow ourselves to rejoice in it!

Laurie, *the owner of Zen Healthy Living for 24 years, is a licensed specialist in Shiatsu therapy and offers hands-on holistic health care specializing in cancer care and support, author of* Journey to the Stage, *international public speaker, and instructor. You can find her at* http://zenhealthyliving.wixsite.com/holistichealth

Chapter Eleven – Laurie Koerselman

"Feel the wind in your hair, the sun on your face, and listen to your inner self roar like the warrior goddess we are meant to be!"

Laurie Koerselman

FOR THE LOVE OF THE WIND IN MY HAIR

I am not a typical female. I have never behaved, fit into any box, colored inside the lines, or always did what I was told. I found the love of the wind in my hair and the sun on my face at age 12 and have craved it ever since.

I lived on a farm with my aunt, uncle and cousins when I first learned to ride. The bike, my cousin Kenny's, was a dark green Yamaha 100 Enduro. I named it Big Green. I rode Big Green up and down every gravel road I could in the area. My best friend lived two miles down the road and I would often go pick her up, and the two of us would ride. The neighbors had a cool apple orchard, and the neighbor girl and I made quite the motocross course between their orchard and our farm. We even had a dirt pile behind the barn to jump our bikes!

I rode Big Green into the nearby small town of 450 people for Driver's Ed at 14 years old. Nobody minded, as country kids would sometimes drive a tractor or snowmobile into town for school. My instructor told me to wear a helmet. I, of course, never did. I loved the feeling of the wind in my hair and on my face!

I rode that bike into high school until I left the farm and moved away. College, jobs, and life filled the days, nights, and years. I rode as a passenger for quite a few years and mostly didn't mind. I still got the wind in my hair! I got my first bike, a Sportster, basically as a divorce settlement when I was 32. I changed the tanks, painted her a black cherry color and called her Roseanna.

Roseanna and I rode the wind as fast as I could most days. I didn't care about tomorrow if I had today to make the most of. Fear was not even a question or thought in my mind. I was fearless, and once again was not behaving or fitting into someone's box. The Sportster took me through till I was 35 when I traded her for a turquoise Softail Custom with lots of chrome that made me drool. One look at that bike and I knew I had to upgrade. I named her Nelly and rode her home on October 25, 2005, in 32-degree weather with snow in the ditches.

Nelly is a head turner, and usually people come up and ask me about her wherever I go. Occasionally I come across a dumb guy who asks if she is mine. *No, I stole it dumbass!* I hear a lot of women that say they would love to ride a bike like that. Little do they realize how much skill it takes to ride Nelly. She has ape hangers, no windshield, and can get a little squirrely sometimes. I've survived an 80 mile an hour wobble on her! That scared me, but my husband reassured me that I was a good rider and should get back in the wind. So, I did, and am glad for it! There is nothing like the feeling of freedom and independence when you are riding your own bike. It is all up to you! I still have Nelly, and she will be given to one of my children someday.

My husband and I had been talking about getting touring bikes so we could take our kids on motorcycle trips. As luck would have it, I found the perfect addition to our collection. I bought my third bike, a teal colored Road King I named Betty, in 2015. She is my favorite bike so far! Maybe it's because I'm getting older or more cautious because I have children. I have a windshield, a sheepskin for my seat, speakers to play Betty's iPod, and yes, now even a cup holder. I now wear a helmet all the time and don't mind it. I try and put 3,000-4,000 miles a year on her.

I have ridden Betty to many places and even challenged myself to ride some scary roads and steel grated bridges (which I still hate) crossing the Mississippi. The older I get, and the more I ride, I still try and challenge myself sometimes. I think it makes me a better rider by improving my skills and pushing those fears away. I would not recommend starting to ride on such a big bike. You have to earn it and respect it.

No matter their age, skill level, and desire, I will always encourage other women to ride. Feel the wind in your hair, the sun on your face, and listen to your inner self roar like the warrior goddess we are meant to be! Don't stay on the porch and listen to your fears, face them head on! Jump outside the box and color outside the lines. The wind is calling you!

Laurie is 48 and rides a 1997 Harley-Davidson Softail Custom and a 2004 Harley-Davidson Road King.

Chapter Twelve – Lynn Cromwell

"Good people are all around, and they seem to be attracted to this sport whether they ride or not."

Lynn Cromwell

GO OUT FOR A RIDE

My partner Rich and I have a game we play during the winter months, or any other time the bikes are parked in the garage and we have a desire to be in the energy of riding but cannot. A few years ago, we decided to stop buying t-shirts as souvenirs of our rides, and we began to purchase decals of the various places we have been to across the United States and Canada. These decals are displayed on the oil tank that is in our garage, and the motorcycles are parked in front of it. We will frequently sit on our bikes and play the game, "Where am I?" often provoked by the memories the decals stir up. One of us usually begins by describing either a person we have met or a place we have traveled without stating the name of the person or place. The other person needs to guess where and who is being described.

Recently, as we were sitting on our bikes bundled up for the cold winter month of January, we began remembering people, and more specifically, non-riding people. Now let me say we will often be told before every trip, "Be careful, there are a lot of crazy people out there." And there are, for sure. It's just we don't tend to run into many. But we have run into some amazingly helpful and generous people. Here are a couple that really stood out for us.

The Mayor
We were entering Sheridan, Wyoming and happened to get caught at a railroad crossing as a train with too many cars

76

to even count was passing before our eyes. As we looked down the tracks, the train looked like it stretched to the horizon. The kickstands went down, the engines were shut off, and we began to stand and stretch alongside our motorcycles. As we did this, the gentleman in the car behind us shut his car off, and noticing we were not from Wyoming he decided to join us and welcome us to the great town of Sheridan, Wyoming! He shook our hands and asked if we were planning to spend the evening, and when we informed him we were he became a cornucopia of information regarding the "best of" Sheridan, Wyoming. This information landed us a reasonably priced hotel, a great meal and one of my favorite pair of riding boots! He may or may not have been the mayor, but to us, he will always be regarded as such!

Kerry on the ferry

Although we had ridden to and stayed in Milwaukee on a previous ride, this was our first time taking the ferry from Muskegon, Michigan. As we boarded the ferry I remembered that I had read something that referred to Lake Michigan as the graveyard of many freighters and boats of all shapes and sizes. My partner and I were discussing these facts, leaning on the railing of the upper deck of the ferry, when a young lady about 20-30 years younger than us politely became a part of our conversation, adding many facts to our concern about the safety of our motorcycles. She explained how the depth, currents and weather of Lake Michigan before the use of radar and more complex navigational equipment caused numerous wrecks and casualties. We learned that she had been born and bred in Milwaukee, and from there the questions and exchange of information ensued. Again, this completely confirmed our belief that when you are on the road, find a local resident and you will find the real best information source. Indeed, Kerry on the ferry was one of those sources!

Don da Don

As usual when we are on the road, we woke, had a cuppa java, and hit the road for 60-100 miles before we stopped to have the first of the two daily meals we usually have on the road. Snack/protein bars always fill a void if needed. So, on this dreary, drizzly day, we pulled into the Country Rose Café where the décor was all things cowboy and the food and java were hot and good. We had just received our meal when a gentleman who we had earlier observed standing and staring at our bikes stood beside our table and inquired if "those two motorcycles out there" were ours. We confirmed his suspicion, and a quick glance around the room proved it was easy to pick us out from the others in the café.

He went on to say, " Please continue to eat. I know you bikers don't like your bikes being dirty, so I arranged to have your bikes washed for you after you eat. Now take your time, and when you are done, just ride through that alley back there, and my buddy will be waiting for you. No money; it's free, I just want to help you out cuz it looks like you two have been riding for quite a bit. Remember, no rush and no money. See ya soon."

And he disappeared. We looked at each other and at the same time said, "Go through the alley back there?!"

But we also looked at the bikes, which cried for a good cleaning, and decided we would check the alley out before riding through it. It turned out the alley wasn't much of one, and sure enough, across from it was a man in his late 20's with a hose in his hand standing in front of one of the garages belonging to a speed shop. And he was waiting for us.

As he got to work on our bikes, Don, who is an avid gardener, gave me a tour of his backyard garden, which is completely hooked up with a 50-year-old sound system softly pumping out seventies rock and roll. What a sweet spot in a dusty western town, and he took such pride in it. Soon, we were not just talking with Don but also the owner of the speed shop, who pulled two stunning choppers out of the garages he had and let us ogle them. What a beautiful job his shop had done on those two bikes. Beautiful, but never practical for our kind of riding.

Two hours later, with our bellies still full, our bikes sparkling clean, and goodbyes shared with our new friends, we were back on the road with the knowledge that there are even more nice people in this world than not, and they make riding all the more special.

So, if your face has been planted in the news and a sense of negativity is hanging over your head, go out for a ride.

Good people are all around, and they seem to be attracted to this sport whether they ride or not.

Lynn *shares that "Against the advice from some experts on how to live a good life, mine has been a series of following my heart. Not always the easiest, let that be said, but certainly filled with laughter and love and all that comes with living a life with heart. So, it is no surprise to me that over lunch with a friend who had lost her job and was selling her motorcycle I entered a world I rarely paid attention to—the world of motorcycle riding.*

Four motorcycles and approximately 130,000 miles of North American roads later, I am thinking, "Thank your life force for giving me the gift of riding. The gifts of my partner, Rich, my two children, Alisha and Derek, seven grandchildren, two dogs, and wonderful friends and family just keeps on giving. And when I need a break from adjunct teaching and working as a mental health therapist I will start that engine and blend into one with my bike, 'Spirit,' a 2017 Street Glide Special."

Chapter Thirteen – Rhonda Wolfe

"I was getting ready to ride my own motorcycle, and I was feeling great!"

Rhonda Wolfe

WHY ROX RIDES

After spending a few of my 'Chapter 2' years riding as a passenger when the opportunity arose, I got tired of waiting for an open back seat to plant myself on. I started searching online for a used bike that would be a good starter for someone who hadn't even been on two wheels since the dirt bike days of my childhood. I spent a few months looking, searching, and reading up on what other women had started out on when they started riding their own.

Fast forward to April 2016, and stepping foot into the local Harley-Davidson dealer here in Centre Hall, PA. To say I was intimidated would be an understatement.

Then I met Lee. Lee wasn't "just a salesman" at #1 Cycle Center Harley-Davidson. He became my champion to get me a bike I could handle, lift when it fell over, and be the starter bike that would work for me! I spent over two hours with Lee as he had me sit on this one and that one, move it around, and jolt it to see how I could handle it.

I explained my extensive back issues and how comfort and weight was a big concern for me. After spending that two-plus hours figuring out this and that, he concluded that the Street 750 would be the best fit for me and I agreed. It had just enough power to scare me, but I could keep up with the big dogs when I was ready to ride. I spent two days poring over my finances to be sure I could afford this baby. I was excited and scared, but I went for it and purchased a

Harley-Davidson Street 750 as my starter bike.

Lee set the bike up very well for me, including the pipes, tuner, and really making sure it was ready for me. The day I went to see it and try it out he took me out back, bike in tow, and we spent a few hours getting me familiar with the entire bike: stop and start, braking, turning vs. leaning (now that I was actually the driver and not the passenger), and how to pick it up if we fell over. Again, he did not even have to do this with me, but it was his reputation on the line and he wanted to absolutely ensure I was going to be ok. April in Central PA is quite rainy, and after an entire week of rain they decided to deliver my bike to me! I was so happy to have that black beauty sitting in my carport just waiting for me to hop on. I would spend an hour or so cruising around my neighborhood, stopping and starting, working figure eights, turning, signaling, all in preparation for the safety course that I was taking in June.

June 2016 was my motorcycle safety course, and I was nervous but excited. I was the only woman in my group of mostly young men, but that didn't intimidate me. I was getting ready to ride my own motorcycle, and I was feeling great! Test day came after the two-week evening course. Guess who was second fastest in the S-turns during the exam? That's right—ME! I passed with flying colors and couldn't wait to celebrate with my friends and family.

There is something about the brothers and sisters who ride, the close-knit community that surrounds being a biker. We participate in rides for charity, raising money for a fallen brother or sister and their families, helping the community as best we can. I never thought that I would belong to such a loving, caring and fun "family." I even started a chapter of an international women's riding club to share my love of riding a motorcycle.

The year 2018 brought a new 'man' in my life, my Storm. He's a 2018 Harley-Davidson Softail Slim, and I am in love! This is my dream bike, and I couldn't be happier. I got Storm at a different dealership but from the same sales guy, Lee, and I got the same fantastic customer services as I did in 2016!

I am so proud to be a woman rider and am sharing that joy with my 16-year-old daughter. She has started to ride with me as of this last summer, and she loves it just as much as I do. Nothing makes me prouder than having my daughter ask to be picked up from school on the bike. She will be a phenomenal woman rider herself one day.

Rhonda, aka Rox, is from Pennsylvania and rides a 2018 Harley Davidson Softail Slim. Rox is the President of the Iron Ladiez Chapter of the Chrome Angelz International Riding Club.

Chapter Fourteen – Sandra M. Graham

"Always a dreamer but also a doer, I just decided one day to take the riders course and get my motorcycle license."

Sandra Morneau Graham

NO OBSTACLE CAN STOP ME

Growing up, I was surrounded by acres of land and gained an appreciation of hard work and nature at its best. My parents owned their own business selling and servicing landscape equipment. At the shop, every day, I would watch my brother John take small engine parts and rewire go-carts and mini-bikes that we would then ride on our property. That grew to snowmobiles, and quad riding later on. I still love the smell of two-cycle engine oil. John eventually had a street bike that I only sat on and pretended to ride. I was soon a passenger on one of our friends' bike, and those are some great memories.

When I was 20, I was in a severe car accident and broke my neck. Doctors worried that I would be paralyzed, but my will to walk overcame that thought. I was walking 11 days after the accident and body surfing in Virginia Beach five months later. That brush with death, as well as others, taught me valuable life lessons, one being not to waste time!

Married, and after having our second child, my husband bought a Harley. Well, I couldn't ride, even as a passenger, with two babies at home. He and his co-workers, friends, and neighbors would ride. Eighteen years passed.

Always a dreamer but also a doer, I just decided one day to take the rider's course and get my motorcycle license. I knew I could ride; my only fear was riding in a group and the highway. I signed up in 2015 and passed. My instructor gave everyone a custom certificate; mine reads

"No Obstacle Can Stop Me." I guess she saw confidence in my riding. I was the only woman in an all-male class, but that didn't bother me. I liked it. Three days later I bought my first bike, a 2015 blacked IRON 883.

I learned fast. The first group ride made sense to me now: ride as a leader and I can set the pace of the ride. Stay in control and ride in your own comfort zone.

My first out of state ride involved some highway. In less than a year after getting my mc license, I gained respect for the road, other drivers, and Mother Nature. Riding in the rain (just do everything the same only slower), riding in the high wind, near and around the updraft from an 18-wheeler, and through flying objects on the highway I learned quickly to take control and be aware of everything around me.

I rode the Sportster for just over a year and hated to give her up. I named her "Black Betty." But I was ready for a bigger bike, one that could take me on long distance rides and had storage—saddlebags are everything when you're on overnight trips. Upon seeing a 2016 Softail Slim S on the showroom floor, I fell in love all over again. It is olive gold (Army green) with the denim finish. It's the WWII replica bike with the big STAR on the tank. I am proud not only to own it but to ride it with pride. At bike rallies that we frequent she's a real conversation piece, like many bikes are.

Whatever you ride, ride the bike that fits you, have fun with it and ride safe. The benefits far outweigh the dangers. Yes, there are dangers in life, but we maneuver through them, don't we? It's 10% fear ~ 90% fun. That's how I roll!

 What really helped me to decide to ride was that I just didn't want to look back on life and say, "I WISH I had," or "I SHOULD have!!!"

 "I DID."

We ride together as a couple, in groups with friends, and I also really love just riding by myself as well. We've ridden all over New England; it has some of the best riding. I also recently rented a Harley while visiting Arizona and had an amazing experience riding through the desert with The Tucson MotoGirls. Next is a ride to and through Nova Scotia this summer.

Get outside and ride!

Sandra grew up in New England and still loves the change of seasons, all of them. She shared that she enjoys travel immensely and wishes to spend more time on her 2016 Harley-Davidson Softail Slim S 110 Screaming' Eagle. Her trips last year included every state in New England, and Nova Scotia and Prince Edward Island, Canada.

Off the road and while not riding, Sandra enjoys her work as a landscape designer and spends most of her time outdoors. Her other interests include, but are not limited to, music, photography, the arts, sewing leather, gardening, pets and staying active.

Sandra and her husband have been married almost 30 years and have two children, who both show interest in street bike riding in their near future. They enjoy seeing the world on two wheels and plan to continue to do so for many years to come.

Sandra shares, "I want to inspire people, in general, to get outdoors, get moving, stay active. Follow your passions, all of them! Having an adventurous spirit, I found one of my greatest passions after the age of 50,—riding motorcycles!"

Chapter Fifteen – Sarah Fisher

"Through the entire trip our communication improved, our patience with each other improved, and our relationship got stronger."

Sarah Fisher

THE ADVENTURES CONTINUE

I started riding in 2015. It was a long journey to get to the point where I dared to get on and twist the throttle. With the utmost support from my husband of 17 years (at that point), I climbed on, twisted the throttle, and never looked back.

The years and miles that followed were beyond amazing. I became more confident in my riding abilities, and we got to travel near and far on our bikes, together but separate. We joked, we got frustrated, hot, wet, windblown, and sunburned. We did it all together, the good and the bad. My growing confidence on my bike helped make me a stronger, more confident woman off my bike. The confidence my husband had seen for some time was coming out, and I was able to see it too.

In 2018 we bought a small pop-up camper to pull behind his bike. The adventures began that spring when he pulled it to a local campground for the weekend. A couple more camping trips with the bike and we were ready for a big test. For our 20th wedding anniversary we decided to ride our bikes and pull the camper to Carlsbad, New Mexico. It had been 20 years of nothing but adventure and we wanted to continue the theme. his new destination was about 950 miles one way, and the goal was to camp every night.

Since he had the camper, I was the lead bike. This was a new experience for me, the "directionally challenged" person that I am, but I was confident that I could lead.

Although I have a navigation system his system is better than mine, so he would talk to me through the intercom, giving me a heads-up that we were turning in a certain number of miles. Through the entire trip our communication improved, our patience with each other improved, and our relationship got stronger. I loved checking my mirrors and seeing him behind me, the entire time knowing he trusted me to watch out for anything ahead of us.

This trip covered just about all the terrain we could hope for—plains, desert, forests, mountains, and some sand. Riding new roads increased my riding confidence more than I had ever imagined. We got to ride different parts of historic Route 66, we saw new wildlife, and we met some interesting people. All those experiences kept up the adventurous theme of the trip.

Yes, we did camp every night. Some days we were exhausted when we set up camp, but we did it. Some mornings started slowly before the coffee kicked in, but we did it. The entire trip was about 3,000 miles of keeping the adventure alive in life and in our relationship. Although I don't ride on the back of his bike any more, motorcycles are still something we do together. And we appreciate each mile.

Sarah rides a 2016 Harley-Davidson Softail Slim S she calls "Eleanor." She is a wife, mom, daughter, sister, and aunt. Sarah and her husband live on a small piece of land in Iowa. She manages an underwriting department. And on evenings and weekends, she hops on her bike.

Sarah shares, "I love seeing the looks on faces when they find out I ride my own bike. Even more than that, I love seeing the young girls wave as I ride by, and encouraging other women to trust themselves to learn to ride."

Chapter Sixteen – Sharon Faith

"My trip was a leap of faith for me into this wonderful world of adventure riding; I have met the most inspiring and encouraging people through sharing the passion for riding."

Sharon Faith

PERU: A SMALL STEP TO A WORLD OF ADVENTURE

Hi, I am Sharon Faith, from Oak Harbor, Washington. It is the largest and most northern city on Whidbey Island, a beautiful place nestled in the cold waters of the Puget Sound. I always feel very lucky to have been born in such an amazing part of the USA.

I have been obsessed with motorcycles from a very early age. I had not had the chance to actually "drive" one then. However, I had been on the back of many and was always watching the controls, wishing, wanting and hoping to own one someday.

Fast forward many years and many lifetimes. One day I was living in Wisconsin, it was approximately 2008, after a difficult time in my life. In my devastation, my girlfriends had rallied around me to help me pull the pieces of my life back together.

One of my "self-esteem" assignments was to write down on a piece of paper all the things I wanted to accomplish. One of the first things on my list was to learn how to ride a motorcycle.

Little did I know that the "devastating" event that I thought had "ended" my life would catapult me into a world beyond my wildest dreams, create a tougher version of the woman that I had already known, and introduce me to the wonderful and magical world of motorcycling!

After the MSF course I moved back to Florida, where I currently reside, and it was here that I purchased my first motorcycle. It was a 2003 Kawasaki Vulcan 500. I had no idea what sort of "biker" I was. So, learning on this bike and riding with whoever I could find was an important part of my journey.

I put 25,000 miles on that bike, which I named Anya, and I discovered after one trip into Georgia and Alabama that my true calling was to be a long-distance, adventure-seeking motorcyclist.

It was after that when I fell in love with the Suzuki V-Strom 650, which is the bike that I have today. I have ridden her about 50,000-plus miles to date.

I am blessed to have discovered a world of adventure riders and met many people who inspire me daily. I have formed friendships where our special bond for adventure, education, and excitement combined with fun and the thrill of the ride, strengthen us all.

I have been riding motorcycles for about 10 years and have been so fortunate to ride in several countries other than the USA. I have rented bikes in other parts of the world, including Nicaragua, Australia, Peru, Bulgaria, Romania, Canada and Mexico, and have ridden too many different types of motorcycles to remember them all, some for a few miles and some for a few weeks.

The Peru trip was important to me as it was my first out of country motorcycle riding experience. It developed, changed and inspired me in many areas of my life and of course most of all in my motorcycle life, which is my main passion.

Motorcycling is a way of life. I have met many people during my years of riding, and I love to discover what made them get into the sport and what inspires them to stay in it. For some, it seems that it was a catalyst to help them through a tough time. Others started a journey of self-discovery and adventure. The type of motorcyclist you are and the reasons that one does it, I have found, are very personal and as different as are the people.

I started my two-wheeled adventures on a Kawasaki Vulcan 500; I rode 25,000 miles all over the states of Florida, Georgia and Alabama in the USA on that bike, and I learned so much about who I am as a woman and a human being, my views on the world, and the power that I can summon within myself to conquer my fears.

I then upgraded to a Suzuki V-Strom 650. It was after that when I learned I was interested in adventure riding. I was then new to this ADV motorcycling world, and when I went to the Overland Expo in Mormon Lake, Arizona, I met the most wonderful people and realized, "I have found my Mothership! Like minds and great adventures…".

Even though I was inspired and encouraged to create my own off road-over land adventure I lacked the experience for such a journey, and I needed to take baby steps to ensure my success, safety, and guarantee a wonderful time.

I had created an adventure/bucket list after I lost my aunt (Susan Demers) to ovarian cancer; she was a huge inspiration in being tough and loving what you can experience. She was a strong supporter of creating the monster that I am today, being an assertive participant in my own life. I decided that all the "Life is Short" stories you hear are true.

I researched Peru, as experiencing the great ancient Inca city of Machu Picchu was on my adventure/bucket list. It seemed a great place to start! I felt like a true adventure would be going to another country, getting completely out of my comfort zone, and challenging my skills and endurance. There were many companies there who offered motorcycling. I wanted a bike smaller than mine back home. I assumed I would probably be falling off a few times since this journey was out of my skill level. I read that most of the journey would be dirt roads and had only just started riding on dirt several months before. I had only a few experiences under my moto boots. So, I wanted a bike that I could pick up. I wanted something light and easy to handle. Also, I had moderate funds and only a couple of weeks to ride, and I wanted something that was at my price point and a reasonable duration.

During my research I had realized that probably the biggest concern I had was drinking the water, so I purchased some Potable Aqua, which are small tablets to make any water safe to drink. Also, being a vegetarian, I have found that Central and South American countries are a blessing in the food department. Overall, with Peru being such a huge tourist destination I felt safe going there.

I discovered Peru Moto Tours, with its owner Alejandro Luna, was based out of Cusco, Peru. This company suited my needs. They offered a variety of motorcycles from 250ccs up to 700ccs. My weapon of choice was the Honda Falcon 400. I had ridden uncharted adventures in the USA, but having a guide who speaks the language and knows the area seemed like a smart idea. One of the many things I have learned from traveling is that the locals always remember the good stuff. I like to call this "the pie and coffee effect." Most locals are very friendly and proud of where they live and are eager to share their knowledge with you.

The planning continued and I investigated the cost of the airfare. It was what I expected for international travel, and the dates were six months away, so I had time to save up some money. I made my decision, which is the first step of an adventure, and then moved forward with the steps to achieve it. For me, once the decision is made the excitement is enough to carry me through with the rest of the planning. I encourage everyone to do some research first before negating the fact that most dreams can be achieved…for everyone.

After waiting what seemed like forever, and carefully packing and repacking of all my motorcycle gear, I was ready to go. I flew from Florida, Jacksonville International Airport to Miami to Lima to Cusco. I arrived the next morning, early.

Alejandro offers an airport pick up service straight to your hotel. It is recommended to arrive a couple of days early. Most people suffer from altitude sickness since Cusco is in the Andes Mountains perched at a lovely 11,200 feet (3,414 meters). I was no exception to this and was very sick my first day. I tried the coca tea but nothing helped me except rest. So that is what I did…quiet rest…and lots of water.

The next day I checked in with Peru Moto Tours and was able to go on an ATV tour that was scheduled and had room for one more. And since I was chomping at the bit to ride my Falcon, they assigned it to me for the next week and let me ride it up to the ATV site. Wow! I was riding a motorcycle in Peru! I was overjoyed with a sense of adventure and freedom. I was practically in tears from excitement about the week to come.

My Falcon, which I named Numero Ocho, was so small and light and awkward at first. I was impressed with the pep and speed of it since it was only 400 ccs. After all the planning and being sick, I was finally riding. It made everything better, as it always does. Immediately I was ready to for whatever life hurled at me. Very surreal.

We rode through dilapidated parts of Cusco, with the smells of roadside eateries, the dogs barking and chasing us, the kids playing in the streets, the traffic—oh, the traffic is not moto friendly—and that made getting out in the country so much sweeter. The air was fresh and crisp, and the sun was shining, that moment where life is perfect from the inside out. That is the part I hunger for every day. That shot of intense perfection, the moment you first have when you realize that you are addicted, and your life is changed forever.

We had a beautiful ride up to the mountains and then a grand tour on the ATV's. As fun as they were, I was only ready for more motorcycling. At dusk we rode back to our hotel , which was right off Cusco main square. Even after dark, the air was charged with the life of a big city in an ancient and beautiful old capital town.

The next morning the tour started, seven glorious days and six nights of traveling by motorcycle and living on the road, my favorite place to be. We started out with a small ride locally; we visited two ruins sites and several towns, one with an ancient church with beautiful decorations. Then we stopped for a coffee and had a bit of time to get to know the other riders.

There were two others on my trip, Daniel from Canada and Matt from the UK. They were like my brothers for the next week. It seems that we were all on this journey for the very same reasons, so we had a love of motorcycling and the desire to witness Machu Pichu in common, which makes for fast friendship no matter what part of the world you are from.

We arrived back late that night and parked our bikes, then off to our rooms to get prepared for our real trip at starting

9 a.m. the next morning. I had a small bag and all my gear. In September it is chilly in the mornings and the days are perfect. I brought my winter gear and a good, full faced helmet, rain gear and good boots, a regular size backpack for a few clothes to change into, a small travel laptop, the camera (of course), a voltage adaptor with a power strip, toiletries, a knife, compass, wet wipes, a few odds and ends, and lots of Chapstick. I also recommend getting small bills of Peruvian money (called Nuevo Soles) for all the various charges on the road, parking, lunches, coffee, and shopping in the outside markets.

My initial desire to go to Peru, like many other people's, was to see Machu Picchu, the ancient Inca city. I have seen photos of this beautiful and magical place from many angles as well as the token tourist "sweet spot" where our guide took us first. I have also watched many documentaries on its history (and speculations about) this special location in our big and beautiful world.

However, the highlight for me was winding through the Andes Mountains on my rented Honda Falcon 400. Our tour covered approximately 850 miles, most of which were hard packed dusty roads.

The people of Peru stole my heart in some of the villages we were able to go through. I was struck by the hardship that Peruvians, in general, had endured for centuries. It shows in the appearances of true Peruvians—each line on their faces is earned with earnest hard work— and by their respect for the environment and Mother Nature. However, they are the most resilient, innovative and creative people. I was in awe of them.

My trip was a leap of faith into this wonderful world of adventure riding. I have met the most inspiring and encouraging people through sharing my passion for riding.

This was a building block for me, increasing my experience, skills, and confidence.

I wonder where the road will take me next....

I am happy to report that since my first adventure my motorcycling journeys continue. My passion for life has, to this day, only increased. Motorcycling is still my favorite way to explore. I know I have many years to come of riding and many adventures waiting for me.

I wonder where the road will take me next...

Sharon currently owns two Suzukis. However, she has been very fortunate to ride many makes and models of motorcycles, and in several parts of the globe.

Chapter Seventeen
Tameka Richardson

"The ride has enhanced my life in many ways. I have gained an extended family that is full of support and love."

Tameka "Kurvez" Richardson

BESSIE STRINGFIELD ALL-FEMALE RIDE

My name is Tameka "Kurvez" Richardson, and I am the creator and chairperson of The Bessie Stringfield All-Female Ride, an annual, three-day motorcycle ride and event for women bikers from across the country. The ride is named in honor of Ms. Stringfield (1911-1993), who was the first known African American woman to ride solo across the continent on a motorcycle. Like Ms. Stringfield, I heard the call of the Harley-Davidson V-twin, and throughout the years and many miles, I have had some of my happiest and most exciting adventures while on two wheels.

Motorcycling keeps me young at heart. I am passionate about sharing the joys of motorcycling with other women. The first big ride I organized was "Divas Cruisin' Da Coast," in 2009. My goal was to unify and inspire women riders from the Gulf Coast states of Florida, Mississippi, Alabama (where I was born) and Louisiana (where I reside now with my family).

My fourth and current motorcycle is a 2017 Harley-Davidson Road Glide Special 1746 cc, a full-dress touring machine that I nicknamed "Blak Ball." I began riding in 2007 on my first bike, a Suzuki GSX-R 750, after experiencing the thrill of riding as a passenger with my boyfriend Franklin for the previous nine years. He is now my husband. Franklin and I are United States Air Force veterans and the proud parents of our son Demetrius, who is currently enrolled in Auburn University. By 2009 I had moved up to an even faster, more powerful bike, the Kawasaki ZX-14.

I briefly flirted with drag racing, but by 2012 I realized that I enjoyed the freedom, relaxation, and camaraderie of cruising on a Harley. I have never looked back. I have ridden across the entire country on my Harley four times, and completed the USA Four-Corner Ride as well as many other long-distance rides, including the Iron Butt endurance race, totaling 115,016 miles to date.

I am following in the footsteps of my idol, Ms. Stringfield, who crisscrossed the country eight times on her Harleys in the 1930's and 1940's.

With the Bessie Stringfield All-Female Ride, I am sharing my passion for my idol and encouraging other women to take to the open road. I believe in leading from the front. I believe that to become an effective leader, you must learn how to follow first. I wouldn't ask anyone to do anything that I'm not willing to do. My life lesson can be summed up in this belief: "It's not how hard you fall, it's how you get back up from the fall." This belief has helped me to be an example to my peers and to stay consistent.

So far, the participants have ridden a total of nearly 7,000 miles in the "Penny Tours," named after Bessie's habit of tossing a penny over a map to choose her destinations. We ride in all weather and put in thousands of miles. Women from across the country converge and participate in pep rallies in various states, where riders are also educated about riding safety and techniques. The sisterhood among the riders is reflected in our exuberance. Just five years ago, there weren't many African American women riding long-distance, nor were we riding cruiser-type motorcycles. In 2014, the Bessie Ride was born, and through Ms. Bessie's legacy a sisterhood filled with diversity and unity was created.

Throughout all these adventures, and being a wife and mother, I have gone to graduate school and earned my Master of Education in Business Education/Marketing at Auburn in 2015, then gone on to earn my teaching certificate. When I'm not out riding or engaged in the many responsibilities that come with being the chairperson of a committee putting on an enormous group ride, I am an educator, teaching high school students (business education and marketing).

The ride committee consists of 10 dedicated women who help coordinate different facets of the ride, from the logistics of destination planning to event coordination, and more. My primary responsibility as chairperson is to ensure that the legacy of Ms. Bessie Stringfield is preserved through research, education, and riding.

Some of my "wind" sisters and myself, began the first Bessie ride with only a handful of women. The 2017 ride had 350 registered participants. In June of 2018, at the Harley-Davidson Museum in Milwaukee, Ms. Stringfield, as well as my ride named in her honor, was recognized with a display case for the event and during the 115th Anniversary for Harley-Davidson.

The theme for 2018 was "We ride for Diversity, Unity, Respect, and Dignity," to continue to unify women bikers to continue the journey in sisterhood. Thus far, the Ride has supported two charities, Hubbard House of Jacksonville, FL (domestic violence) and Mo's Heroes (homeless veterans), with many more planned for the future.

The ride has enhanced my life in many ways. I have gained an extended family that is full of support and love. I have also met and ridden with a diverse group of women and men that I would have never met otherwise. Although there are moments when it appears that my thoughts are never-ending, and there are sleepless nights while preparing for an event or road trip, I wouldn't trade it for the world. It has truly become a "labor of love."

For more information on the Bessie Stringfield All-Female Ride, check out our website, www.bessiestringfieldallfemaleride.com.

Tameka is a high school business education and marketing teacher. She is also the creator and chairperson of Bessie Stringfield All Female Ride, Inc., Creator/Chairperson. Tameka lives in Louisiana with her husband, Franklin. Their son Demetrius is a student at Auburn University. She currently rides a 2017 Road Glide Special

Chapter Eighteen
Tina Desruisseaux

"My motorcycle has become my source of new life to breathe and an inspiration to so many other women who want to ride, but don't want to go it alone or fear they can't do it."

Tina Marie Desruisseaux

THE HORIZON NEVER ENDS, I CONQUERED
MY DREAM TO RIDE

At the age of 47, I found my life taking a journey to the unknown and had to come to terms that I may walk my life with my now five-year-old rescue dog, Gracie. As I reflected on my life, I realized my passion was to get a Harley and ride.

At the age of 49 I bought a 2002 Sportster with only 8,000 miles on her. She was a dream starter bike, and she sounded throaty. I had to have her. I then remembered that my dad had shared with me that I had climbed on his chopper at the age of two, and at that point in my life I knew he had created a future wind sister!

I had one thing left to do, and that was to get my license. One week after purchasing my motorcycle, I had my license in hand. I was in awe and the only thing that went through my head during that is moment was, "Thank you, Daddy, you set this dream in my head at the age of 2 and here I am 49, standing proud! The only thing missing is the little girl you raised wants to have one day to ride beside you."

As I ventured out for my very first ride as a solo single woman, I had many thoughts going through my head. "Is this for real? Can I go one gear down and remember all the rest are up from there?" Once I went from first gear and wrapped my brain around "now into second gear," I truly knew that when I squeezed in that clutch and geared into second, I would feel the power of freedom within myself! I had a smile so big I thought I was going to crack my face. I felt so confident in all the skills I learned in taking the MSF safety course that I knew there was no stopping me at this point.

My first ride was out to the coast from NH to Maine, and all I remember was my happiness and my soul reaching for peaks I never felt possible.

My motorcycle has become my source of new life and an inspiration to so many other women who want to ride, but who don't want to go it alone or fear they can't do it. I have encouraged other women to ride, conquer their fears, and achieve their dreams. It's become my best circle of friends, and it continues to grow. I sold my Sportster this summer to a wonderful lady who had the dream to ride and wanted something she would love. She started up my Sportster, and when I saw that smile on her face I knew I was gaining another friend, another wind sister. Three days later she picked up the Sportster, and on June 13th of 2018 I brought home my new to me 2005 Harley Soft-tail Deluxe. Not only do I ride with my friend who bought my Sportster, but I also ride with other women I have met thru the ladies of our HOG chapter.

When I am approached by other females who don't ride but dream of riding, I encourage them to follow their dream for the freedom. I am my own person with the will to continue to grow, and the wind in my face keeps me focused and the road ahead with hills and turns keeps me looking forward to my next ride. When I look in my rearview mirror, I hope one day to see another female rider join the family, for the love of riding is like no other! When I am on my motorcycle and a child waves to me, I know the passion lies within them, and one day they may have the gift to ride and build a dream they never thought possible.

Being a single woman has pushed me to the highest levels of confidence due to my love for riding. I am now 51, and though my Dad and I will never ride together, he is my guardian angel, and he continues to look down on me and watch me grow and build friendships with other riders. Gracie and I will one day ride together as my next journey is to put goggles and a helmet on her and get a motorcycle with a sidecar. I ride with the wind in my face and give thanks to the horizon that never ends.

PEACE.

Tina *was born and raised in New Hampshire. She rides a 2005 Softail Deluxe. Tina shares that "My daughter isn't a fan of motorcycles, but because it's my passion she now wants to ride on the back of my motorcycle at the age of 32…it's so inspiring to others as I ride and love my journey." Tina is an account dedicated appeals manager in behavioral health services for a Fortune 500 health insurance company. She is 51 years old, divorced, with two beautiful children, daughter Nichole, son-in-law Keith, son Tyler and her sweet loving granddaughter Naomi. Naomi is three years old and she gets Harley clothes from gramma Tina :).*

Chapter Nineteen – Tina Simpson

"We've met some awesome people and have made lifelong friends along the way."

Tina Simpson

RIDE SAFE–A MOTORCYCLE SAFETY COURSE IS A MUST!

My first experience was in the '60's on a Honda 90 on a dirt track beside my uncle's Honda shop. I was 10 or 12 years old. Then in the early 70's my Dad and my best friend's dad each purchased Rupp 50s. My friend and I rode those things all over town. Boy, did we think we were cool!!!

Then life happened, and I didn't ride for many years. I divorced, and in 1987 I married again. My new husband had a motorcycle but didn't ride much. We owned a 24-hour business that in the beginning kept us very busy, and we eventually sold it.

A few years later we bought a 1997 Kawasaki 1500 Vulcan Classic. He joined the VROC (Vulcan Owners and Riders Club). The club meets each year in the fall in Arkansas, the same weekend as Bikes, Blues and BBQ. In 1998 the National Meet was in Durango Colorado on Labor Day weekend at the Four Corners rally. We began to ride to Durango each year for Labor Day weekend and to Eureka Springs in late September.

My husband constantly encouraged me to get my own bike, partly because he thought I would enjoy it but also because he just wanted me off his bike. He came home one day with a small bike (I don't remember what it was) and said, "Here's your bike. Now you can learn to ride."

I wasn't sure I wanted my own bike. However, he didn't give up so I started to ride, mostly in parking lots. I upgraded to a Honda Shadow 600 and took the motorcycle test at our local DMV.

Then my husband bought a 2003 Kawasaki 1500 Nomad and gave me his hand-me-down Classic. The Classic was set up for him (he's 6'1"), but I (5'6") rode it for two years. I was on tippy toes when I put my feet down. I rode scared, didn't like to lean, didn't like riding in traffic, and rode slow.

It was not a good time. I am completely surprised we are still married! I dropped it several times and once threw myself over the handlebars because I grabbed the front brake too hard. I kept riding, though. I love to ride. I just wanted to ride slowly with no traffic.

One Labor Day weekend on our way to Durango we stopped for fuel. I told him, "If you want me to continue to ride with you I'm getting a bike that I like, that fits me."

I had always liked the Indian motorcycles. However, one wasn't available at that time. A Kawasaki Drifter looked to be the next best thing. My husband said, "Buying a bike is like buying a dress, you've got to try it on because if it doesn't fit you're not going to wear it." So, I set out to "try one on." We'd met a couple from Arizona in Durango, and she rode a Drifter. I asked if I could ride it around the parking lot, and she graciously said yes. I was in love with the ride as much as I was the looks. We came home and immediately started to look for a Drifter. We found a 2004 (with only 350 miles) on e-Bay. I had the bike in time for our late September trip to Arkansas.

The next summer, two of my cousins-in-law (sisters) invited me to go on a girl's motorcycle trip. When I talked to my husband about it, he said "YES! Go." And so off we went to South Dakota. We didn't have any definite plans, we just rode, stopped along the way when we wanted to, and got a hotel when we were done for the day. We saw all the sites. We had a blast and made the trip without any problems or incidents.

On one ride home from Durango my bike wasn't running right, so my husband and I traded bikes. After a few miles we traded back. He said, "Keep it above 80, you'll be fine." So, down the road we went. It was late in the day. We were heading east. The sun was setting and shining directly on the back of his bike. He signaled to turn, but I didn't see it because of the sun.

I couldn't slow down in time. I didn't think to swerve around him, and I hit him. I caught his left saddlebag with my right footboard. We stopped, he yelled, I cried, we picked up the pieces and strapped them down, and rode home. Thankfully no one was hurt, and the bikes could be fixed.

Shortly after that, I took the Motorcycle Safety Course with a friend. We enrolled in the one-day class and rode our own bikes. The class ended up being ALL GIRLS, and it RAINED. In that riding condition you want to learn from the best. What a difference that one day class made in my riding ability!

In 2014 I sold my Drifter with 50,000+ miles on it and bought my dream bike, an Indian. I thought I wanted the Indian Vintage. I really like that "old" Indian look. However, again I had to "try it on" and ended up getting the Chieftain. We lowered it a bit, and it fits perfectly. I bought it from a dealer in Oklahoma in February and it was too cold to ride home, so we trailered it. Our friends made fun of me for trailering it. Now my nickname will forever be "Sissy."

Two years ago we rode the Tail of the Dragon in Robbinsville, NC. What a blast! We're lucky to have good friends close by that also ride. I've been to North Dakota, South Dakota, Wyoming, Montana, Nebraska, Oklahoma, Missouri, Kentucky, Tennessee, North Carolina, Colorado, Arkansas, Florida, Texas, and of course all over Kansas. We've met some awesome people and have made lifelong friends along the way.

Tina is from Kansas and is 61 years young! Tina is self-employed and owns an oil field service company. She has four grown children (three girls and one boy), and six grandchildren (three girls, three boys). Tina rides a 2014 blue Indian Chieftain.

Chapter Twenty - Tracey Byrne

"Feeling so chuffed and proud of myself, riding home on a high, realizing I am gradually conquering my fears."

Tracey Byrne

FINDING MY TRIBE

My name is Tracey. I am a 57-year-old mother of 6 and grandmother of 7. I live in a very small rural community in Central Queensland, Australia, where I work as a teacher's aide in our tiny school of only nine students (this year). I ride a beautiful white Kawasaki Z300 and still own my Kawasaki KLX250.

After having my learners permit since the 1990s, I finally got my motorbike license on the 12th August 2017 at the tender age of 56 (I turned 57 one month later). I asked the instructor if I was the oldest person she had ever tested. I really thought I was the oldest to get a bike license. But I have found many lady riders who are my age or older than me and younger than me, and just recently I met a 60-year-old man on a motorbike learner permit.

My first bike was a Kawasaki KLX250. I learned to ride on this bike and got my license on it, but it isn't a pretty bike. I read a comment somewhere, "when you get off your bike and walk away, if you look back at it, and can't say 'that's a fine-looking bike,' then it's the wrong one for you." So, I bought myself a white Kawasaki z300 and named her Naked Ninja. Now, when I look at my bike, I say, "isn't she beautiful?" I bought a white helmet, and I put Ninja Nanna on it because I have a black belt in Taekwondo and I am a nana. With a white jacket as well, I hope that makes me more visible on the road as safety is important to me when riding.

I wanted to write my story in the hope it might inspire other ladies who might be considering learning to ride, but think they are too old or just not confident, to just go and do it.

My only regret is I wish I had got my motorbike license earlier.

My husband was my high-school sweetheart. But when we graduated from high school we went our separate ways. Twenty-one years later in 1999, we met up again, both of us single parents. He has been riding motorbikes since the '80's and has been my number one supporter, encouraging me to get my bike license once I made the decision to "just do it." He rode with me for what probably seemed like an eternity for him.

I had a few setbacks while learning to ride, dropping the bike many time and breaking my foot on one occasion, putting me out of action for a couple of months, having to cancel my first booking to take the riding test because of my injury. Also, the death of one of my brothers in a light plane crash and his funeral being held on the day I had rebooked my riding test led to me canceling again. Finally, I did the Q-ride test and passed. I am not sure who was happier, my husband or myself.

Now I was able to ride without a support rider with me. I was really nervous, but I made myself put on my riding gear and just get on that bike and ride the 50 kilometers into the closest big town.

Initially, I mostly rode alone or with my husband, because I didn't know any lady riders. So, I googled female riding groups, joined many Facebook pages for lady riders. I read as much as I could, trying to learn how to ride safely, and hoped to find another lady to ride with.

Early in 2018 I decided to ride with a group I had joined on Facbook. It was a huge disappointment for me because they rode off and left me behind before the ride even started. Luckily, my husband stayed with me. Humiliated, embarrassed, and really doubting myself and my riding ability, I decided not to ride with a group again.

My husband and I did a couple of long rides together, and I tried very hard to get my speed up. One ride was almost 450 kilometers in a day. My confidence was slowly gaining momentum again.

About six weeks later another group ride was happening. Riders from three towns joined for a large group ride. It was well organized with a lead rider and a back rider. We did approximately 350 kilometers that day, and I kept up with the group. My chest was bursting with pride. My confidence was growing. Hubby was so proud of me; he bought a bottle of wine to celebrate my first successful group ride.

In the meantime, a local ladies group had just formed on Facebook, and I was one of the first members. It was amazing how quickly this group grew. There was obviously a great need for a lady riders' group in our area. One week after my first successful group ride and two weeks after the lady riders' group started, I went on my first ladies-only ride. There were 12 riders with one being a learner and two more meeting us at our destination. We had a lead rider, a lady who stayed back for new or nervous riders (like me), and a sweeper to make sure we didn't miss any turnoffs. I did 374 kilometers that day. No one judged anyone for what they rode. One lady rides a maxi scooter, and she kept up with no problems at all. The ladies were all beautiful souls, encouraging, and just made the ride the best I have been on so far. We rode a steep winding range (which I was quietly nervous about initially), stopped for group photos, and went to a bakery for morning tea. There was lots of laughter, sharing of stories, and getting to know each other better.

Then we toured the historic rural town of Mount Morgan. We rode home via a road they call the Razorback. The name worried me, and the description of the downward incline made me nervous. I asked one of the ladies to ride behind me in case I panicked. I successfully rode the Razorback. Feeling so chuffed and proud of myself, riding home on a high, I realized I am gradually conquering my fears.

I believe in facing my fears and try very hard not to let fear stop me from doing things. It's amazing how many times I realize I had nothing to fear but fear itself.

I love the comradery of the biker community, especially the ladies. The waves and the nods as riders pass each other. The looks of surprise and approval when guys realize you're a female rider. The sense of belonging. I do believe you need to find a group suitable for you to ride with, and I believe I have found that group now. A lady on Facebook told me "you need to find your Tribe." I think I found my Tribe last weekend on our inaugural ladies-only ride.

The future of riding is looking good. I have my husband to ride with, the lady riders' group, and other long rides planned as well as solo rides. My big goal for 2018 is to ride 1,200 kilometers to the Mega Babe Raid (lady riders only) in Dubbo, New South Wales, Australia in November. I have booked our tickets, so I can't chicken out now. It is three days of babe raiding. Two days are ladies only, and on the third day supporters can help and participate in some world record attempts. My husband is riding with me as a supporter. The trip to Dubbo will be approximately 2,400 kilometers of riding in total, including getting there and then back home. I am nervous and excited. Some of the ladies I have met online from all over Australia will be attending as well, and I am looking forward to meeting them in person.

So, I will finish my story with my favorite riding phrase at the moment: -"never ride faster than your angel can fly."

Tracey *is a mother of six children and has seven grandchildren so far. She lives in a small rural community in Queensland, Australia, where she works as a teacher's aide in their tiny local school of nine children. Many years ago she started training with a taekwondo club, and after a few years, she earned her first degree black belt. She hopes that by writing her story people can see they can do anything they want to, whether they are male or female, young or old. She says, "If you set your mind to it, you can do anything." She rides a* Kawasaki Z300 *and still owns her Kawasaki KLX250.*

Chapter Twenty-One
Joan Krenning

"This journey has been a journey of self-discovery... a journey filled with adventure, uncertainty, and unlimited possibilities."

Joan Krenning

A JOURNEY OF SELF DISCOVERY

Aslight breeze pushed back my hair as I slid off my Shubert helmet and swung my leg over and off of my sweet Freedom Glide a 2013 Street Glide. I ran my fingers through the dampness of my hair, closed my eyes and allowed that moment to consume me. As my eyes opened slowly, the vastness of the Black Canyon, located just 11 miles south of the Hoover Dam on Arizona Hwy 93, spread out in front of me. Its beauty was simply undeniable. The vastness and the power of this moment touched me like none other. The time was 3 p.m. The odometer registered 49,820, just 180 miles shy of the 50,000 mile mark, on a journey I had set out on February 4th, 2013. I had been on the road for 21 months and 10 days.

Leaning in

When the moments I refer to as *remarkable* take place, I feel so humbled. Allowing myself to be led by these nudges from God has opened me up to many incredible experiences. I have never been disappointed. What took place next could only have been scripted by One.

I left Las Vegas too late that afternoon to reasonably make the 225-mile ride before dark. As I rode, I opened myself up to what was happening and carefully paid attention to the many signs along the way. And I did receive the bonus, the miracle, the sign from above that the path that I was on was perfect.

Pulling back onto Hwy 93 I headed south towards
Kingman. The ride was exquisite, that late afternoon
November weather perfect for riding.

Paying attention

Ninety miles down the road I pulled into Kingman,
stopped for gas, and went inside for a bite to eat. I texted
my best friend, Rock, and asked if he could find me a room
in Ash Fork, AZ. My destination on Saturday was
Cottonwood, AZ and I needed to be in there by 1 p.m. By
the time I had ridden through Kingman to the other side,
the sun was setting and a chill had definitely set in. Aww,
riding in the desert in the winter.

Once again I pulled off the road, this time to "gear up."
The text on my phone said, "You really don't want to stay
in Ash Fork, AZ. Both motels have bars on the windows."
It was from Rock. My answer back was, "That's OK. I
have stayed in worse."

Preparing for wonder

With 85 miles to go, I was now in for the most profound
experience of my entire 50,000 mile ride—riding east and
following the beauty of the setting sun in my rear view
mirror and watching as the most beautiful full moon rose
over the mountains ahead of me, simultaneously.
Cruising at about 65 mph, I was in the zone, riding solo in
my own little world. Exiting at Ash Fork, I stopped for a
moment just to absorb the moment, and then pulled into
the heavily graveled parking lot of the Ash Fork Inn.

Just inside the door, my eyes did a wide sweep as I took in the immediate surroundings. The lobby decor was a complete Route 66 look. The 80-year old woman behind the counter smiled widely as I walked into the door, appearing very tired and road worn.

"You must be Lady Road Dog," she said as I approached the counter.

"I can see my 'chief of staff; did a great job of tooting my horn," I replied as I laughed.

She informed she had been there for over 30 years as she checked me in, making me feel extremely welcome.

The reward

To the right of the counter hung a poster of James Dean, saying, "Dream as if you'll live forever. Live as if you'll die today."

Back outside I kicked the Freedom Glide in gear to pull up to my $28 room, which was the best the town had to offer. I looked down to switch off my Glide and the odometer read, 50,000 miles exactly!

After nearly 22 months and 50,000 miles, at 10 p.m. on a Friday evening in Ash Fork, Arizona, in a cheap motel beneath the full moon, I opened the door and hanging right in front of me was a framed Successories poster on the wall. It showed a highway leading into the distance, captioned **GOALS: Effort and courage are not enough without purpose and direction.** Successories posters are often hung on the walls of corporate America, but never in $28-a-night, flea bag motels.

The invitation: God sent me on a road trip traveling 50,000 miles to send me an invitation.

> The invitation of Jesus is a revolutionary call to fight for the heart of humanity. We are called to an unconventional war using only the weapons of faith, hope, and love. This war is no less dangerous than any war ever fought. And for those of us who embrace the cause of Christ, the cost to participate in the mission of God is nothing less than everything we are and everything we have. - Erwin Raphael McManus

Isn't this how life is supposed to work...as an ADVENTURE, a JOURNEY, a ride filled with uncertainty, excitement, and risk?

This journey has been a journey of self-discovery...a journey filled with adventure, uncertainty, and unlimited possibilities. It has been a journey of freedom...it has been a journey of joy! This journey has also been a journey of change, of being open to discovery and watching for the signs.

I am all in. Twenty-nine years ago I gave my heart to the only One who can bring me fully alive, to love Him with simplicity and intensity, to unleash the untamed faith that has nestled inside my heart,. to be consumed by His presence, to live as passionately and compassionately as God, and to go where He sends me, no matter the cost.

Living with renewed passion,

Joan aka Lady Road Dog, *Director of Adventure Steel Horse Sisterhood left February 4th, 2013, to embark upon a three-year motorcycle tour called Glory USA Freedom Ride. Her personal mission was simple: to inspire hope in Americans. She rides a 2013 Street Glide.*

Her story is one of a path to significance paved by old sins, shaped by adversity, and driven by courage, faith and true grit. According to Joan, it is ONLY through riding the roads she's ridden that she has realized her life's mission of becoming S.T.R.O.N.G.; smart, tenacious, radical, outrageous, natural, and graceful.

Joan's life story, Driven, Yet Guided, is one woman's journey on the road to redemption and true freedom. You will laugh, cry and love with Joan as you relate to her each of her seven "life altering moments." Driven, Yet Guided, will be released in the fall of 2019.

She is a visionary and a champion of women; the creator of DesignWraps and the founder of S.T.R.O.N.G. Women, a movement which began in the heart of the Rocky Mountains. Joan lives in Arizona close to her family.

The Beginning - Sarah Andreas

Many books conclude with The End…but this one, just like the first *Women Who Ride* book concludes with The Beginning. The beginning of *your* adventures, of you taking charge of your life, goals and dreams, and making them become part of your reality. For many women, riding motorcycles becomes part of their DNA.

I hope that you enjoyed reading the stories as much as I enjoyed collecting them for this book. I truly enjoyed the connection that I built with each of the contributors. I have made many new friends who I hope to meet in person over the next couple of years. These women are amazing!

Each woman who has contributed to this book reflects courage, a love of life and themselves. They filled me with gratitude and I am honored to be able to present them through the writing and publishing of this book.

I hope that their stories have inspired you to embrace the journey!

Sarah Andreas

Meet The Author

Sarah Andreas has a passion for women who ride. She believes that they show strength, passion and courage. She shares that her passion for riding came when she worked for five Harley-Davidson dealerships for just over 13 years before leaving to pursue a career as a leadership development consultant, speaker and author.

As the founder of WiseWood LLC, her purpose in life is to teach, research, coach and write about leadership development.

Sarah has a Master of Business Administration degree from Malone University and a Doctor of Philosophy in Organizational Leadership from Johnson University. She uses these skills to help her clients identify their current state, their desired future state, and develop a strategic plan to move forward on their career journey.

Her first book, *Career Advancement Strategies for Emerging Leaders*, was released in 2016. It was written to help young professionals identify the simple things that could hold them back in their career.

Women Who Ride: Rebel Souls, Golden Hearts and Iron Horses was released in 2018, and you must read the second edition. Sarah lives on a 250+ acre farm in Strasburg, Ohio, with her husband Dan and their son Marcus. Yes, she knows how to drive a tractor and rides a Harley-Davidson motorcycle!

Sarah often shares an African proverb: "If you want to go fast, go alone, if you want to go far, go together." Sarah believes that by building and maintaining relationships we can create growth and development for everyone. It is this belief that started Sarah on the journey to write *Women Who Ride*.

Contact Sarah via email at sarah@wisewoodllc.com.

Meet The Editor

Thishis book is an anthology and it gets its beauty from the people who participate in creating it.

Julie Webb moved to the mountains of Mexico twenty years ago, where she delights in both seasons—the one with rain and one without—and the complete absence of snow and ice.

Her passion for the written word spurred Julie to earn a degree in English, and her love of helping writers led to a career lasting over thirty years as an editor and proofreader. "Fiction, nonfiction, spiritual, inspirational, educational, humorous—I love it all!" she shares. "Working with new authors and seeing their joy when their first book is published is very rewarding. It's also inspiring to work with authors who go on to write multiple books and watch as their confidence and writing careers develop."

Visit Julie's website at https://editorjulie.weebly.com/ or email her at editorjulie@yahoo.com.

Do you want to contribute to the next edition?

Email author@womenwhoridebook.com

INCLUDE:
• your suggested submission title.
• up to 1,000 word true story about you and your motorcycle adventures
• your name, and the make and model of your motorcycle.
• your email address and phone number.

If your submission has previously been published, please include the name of the publication and confirm that you have the publication's permission to reprint the article elsewhere.

RELEASE DATE: check the website, womenwhoridebook.com, and visit the Facebook page at: https://www.facebook.com/womenwhoridebook/.

COPYRIGHT: Original stories, quotations and tributes remain the property of and copyright is held by the contributor. There is NO FEE to participate in this publication and NO OBLIGATION to purchase printed books. NO royalties are paid for selections accepted for publication.
Books are published through WiseWood, LLC.